*Other books by John Heron*


Feeling and Personhood
Sage Publications, 1992

Co-operative Inquiry
Sage Publications, 1996

Sacred Science
PCCS Books, 1998

The Complete Facilitator's Handbook
Kogan Page, 1999

Helping the Client
Sage Publications, 2001

Cosmic Psychology
Endymion Press, 2006

Living in Two Worlds
Endymion Press, 2006

# Participatory Spirituality

*A Farewell to Authoritarian Religion*

John Heron

## Lulu Press

Morrisville ◊ North Carolina

First edition

Published and printed by:

Lulu Press Inc.
800 Aviation Parkway
Suite 300
Morrisville
North Carolina 27560
USA

Participatory Spirituality: A Farewell to Authoritarian Religion

ISBN  978-1-84728-793-9

*The photo on the front cover and the graphic images on pages i,  55, 65 and 162 by John Heron.*

This book is dedicated with love and gratitude to Anne, Annie, Barbara, Bill, Glenn, Gregg, Kim, Ksenija, Selina, Trisha, Rex and Roger, who are my colleagues in our ongoing spiritual inquiry group at the South Pacific Centre for Human Inquiry.

# Perspectives

# Preface

This book is a distant relative of David Hockney's photo collages, in which he presents together many different overlapping photos of the same scene taken from different points of view and at different times. The effect is to enhance the spatiality of the scene, combined with a sense of temporal narrative within it, of movement through it and a dynamic comprehensive participation in it.

Here I have conceptually joined together a number of discrete texts each of which presents a view of human spirituality as participating co-creatively in the life divine. The diverse Perspectives of the overlapping views include passages of related or identical text, in each case set within a different frame of view. A variety of lenses are used: the manifesto; the personal story; theology; metaphysics; epistemology; pathology; psychology; practice. Some Perspectives are wide aperture views; some focus on particular segments; some are short, some are longer. Some have never been seen before, some have been on my website, and some have been published in a book or journal, which is cited at the end of the relevant chapter.

The Perspectives are numbered for ease of reference. Perspective 6 is the view toward a key co-ordinating vanishing-point, so it is a good place to start, followed by Perspectives 8 to 11 which are at the centre of the conceptual collage. But there really is no prescribed sequence for reading the text. In viewing a photo collage, you focus first on a photo which draws your attention and move in the spirit of free exploration from photo to photo while deepening your appreciation of the whole. So with this book, start with any topic that takes your fancy and move thereafter unconstrained from place to place.

In this way the book invites you to engage with it in a participatory manner, to co-create it with your own uninhibited spontaneity. To support this adventurous roaming of the actual text, I have made it index-free. An index is a list of entries devoid of context.

The book also invites you to appropriate any of its contents in any way that clarifies or contributes to your own autonomous worldview, including the presentation of your beliefs to others. To this end, I have abandoned a conventional copyright approach in favour of unrestricted rights of reproduction and use by anyone. See the disclaimer on the copyright page.

The subtitle of this book, *A Farewell to Authoritarian Religion*, is intended to convey a respectful departure from the traditional authoritarianism of spiritual schools ancient and modern.

*John Heron*
Kaukapakapa, September, 2006

# 1 Prologue: a participatory spiritual culture

An increasing number of spiritually-minded people are currently busy with their own lived inquiry, and are seeking open and constructive dialogue about it. I call this social phenomenon, with which I closely identify, a newly emerging and participatory spiritual culture. It involves a growing and significant minority of people across the planet.

We are a loose, informal network of individuals and groups who are shaping our own spiritual paths from the creative wellspring within, evolving new forms appropriate to our day and age. At the same time, we honour and draw on, selectively and adaptively, the vast data bank of spiritual practices and beliefs derived from a diversity of sources, ancient and modern, worldwide.

My sense of it is that there are three interrelated criteria which, applying in varying degrees to any one individual, identify us:

- We affirm our own original relation to the presence of creation, find spiritual authority within and do not project it outward onto teachers, traditions or texts.

- We are alert to the hazards of defensive and offensive spirituality, in which unprocessed emotional distress distorts spiritual development, either by denying parts of one's nature, or by making inflated claims in order to manipulate others.

- We are open to genuine dialogue about spiritual beliefs and to collaborative decision-making about spiritual practices undertaken together.

The term 'participatory' applies to this culture in two intimately connected ways. First, we participate in the living spirit autonomously, in the light of our own discriminating awareness. And second, we participate in the living spirit co-operatively, sharing presence, and learning how to make decisions together about the forms of our spiritual culture that celebrate both our diversity and our unity.

This simple and radical combination bids farewell to authoritarian religion, in which an external authority prescribes the limits within which spiritual autonomy and co-operation may be exercised.

*1*

# 2 The life divine and innovative spirituality

## An open-ended, innovative spirituality

I give here a short account of the kind of spiritual innovation with which 'we' want to engage. The 'we' here refers to all those whose vision is broadly aligned with the content of this Perspective.

## We value affiliation, abundance, challenge and inquiry

1. We value basic forms of association which bring us regularly together with friends who share our aspirations. We value affiliation and togetherness in order to do things in harmony with others, to reach out to each other, and to enjoy each other.

2. We value the expression of praise, an overflowing of the soul with a celebration of the abundance of life and the challenge of life. We seek to integrate the art of expansive enjoyment with the art of transformative suffering.

3. We value shared inquiry, an exploration of the many dimensions of the life divine through sacred, imaginative and playful experiment, discriminating experience and active enterprise.

## We choose a comprehensive spiritual hypothesis

We choose, as a working hypothesis for lived experiential inquiry, to construe the life divine in all the following ways:

1. It is inclusive of this world; there is nothing here which it does not embrace. The very texture of everyday life participates in it. The divine has imaginative, dramatic, passionate and sensuous expression in our immediate experience of this world. In every situation it is the presence between.

2. It is deeply interior to this world, an immanent, ecstatic source, a well-spring that we can contact in the living ground of our embodied experience.

3. It is ineffably beyond this world. The world and our experience does not exhaust it; it forever emanates and transcends all our realities and all our categories.

4. It can, in its different aspects, have androgynous, female, and male attributions.

5. It is inclusive of, and within and beyond, subtle, higher frequency worlds - with their indwelling powers and presences - behind and interpenetrating the veil of this one. We are committed to take account of these other worlds and inquire into their influence on our lives in this world.

## 3) We value a spiritual affirmation of personhood

We take an affirmative view of the individual human being in a spiritual context, and it is expressed in the following set of working hypotheses:

1. Each individual soul is a unique creation of the life divine, and is born into this world which offers it a radical environment for personal, social and ecological development through creative endeavour, learning and inquiry.

2. The soul is a potential person and can, through the circumstances of birth, social influence and education, develop into an actual person with a distinct identity.

3. A person is someone who is learning how to be creatively autonomous, imaginatively self-directing in their life, with beliefs and values to the meaning and practice of which they are internally committed.

4. A person is someone who is learning how, in all areas of living, to co-operate in creative enterprises with other persons without colluding with them; and learning how to support and facilitate, on a reciprocal and peer basis, the development of each individual's potential for personhood.

5. A person is someone who is learning how to be self-transfiguring: how to participate in wider reaches of reality in the subtle worlds; how to be open to here and now situational presence; how to manifest the divine within, and refract the divine beyond; and how to express all this in the transformation of earthly life.

6. The distinctness of personal identity is inalienable. It can be affirmed, celebrated and enhanced to an unlimited degree. It can be transfigured by the spiritual life; it cannot be eliminated by it. It can get woefully lost in, and confused with, egoic separateness, alienation and confusion: but it can, in principle, always be recovered and redeemed.

7. Personal identity is intensified by the change of physical death; personal learning continues in the subtle worlds, which are dramatic in the vast scope of their possibilities.

8. The communion of persons together, sharing presence with each other and their divinity, is an essential need for created souls, a fundamental source of inner sustenance, growth, delight and peace. This inward and spiritual intercourse can also include, through appropriate ritual, persons in the subtle worlds.

## We value a culture of collaborative inquiry

As persons who are in a process of continuous creativity, learning and development, we choose a society whose forms are consciously created and adopted, periodically reviewed, and altered in the light of experience, reflection and deeper vision. We call this a self-generating culture. This is a culture whose forms its members continually recreate through cycles of collaborative living inquiry. It has several strands. As developing persons:

1. We want to explore the use of three basic modes of decision-making - deciding autonomously by oneself, deciding co-operatively with others, and deciding hierarchically for others - so that in different sorts of association we can combine and balance them in different forms. These forms are adopted intentionally, subject to periodic review, with an accepted procedure for changing them. This same conscious learning process is equally applicable to all the points that follow.

2. We want to explore different forms of association in daily living and working, so that we can find various ways of balancing the claims of being and doing things - alone, together with others, or beside others.

3. We want to explore the where and how of housing: private dwellings in the existing urban and rural set-up; private dwellings in a communal village; co-habitation in a communal building; different forms of ownership and rights of use.

4. We want to explore new behaviours in, and beliefs about, a wide range of social roles: woman, man, parent, child, teenager, adult, aged, friend, citizen, and many more.

5. We want to explore forms of economic organization, and of job definition, in order to choose awarely different ways of distributing and combining the roles of owner, manager and worker; and different forms of income and wealth distribution.

6. We want to explore ways of caring for the planetary environment, sustaining and enhancing its dynamic eco-system: covering energy, technology, agriculture, pollution, etc. As part of this enterprise, we

want to research the structure and processes in this world in the context of their interrelation with the structure and processes in subtle worlds.

7. We want to explore forms of providing for children and young people of all ages: how they are to be cared for, raised and educated, and by whom. Also forms of education and training for the personal and professional development of adults; methods for dealing with individual and social overload of emotional distress, and for deep levels of pain and suffering.

8. We want to explore ways of giving social form to spiritual, emotional and physical intimacy, to nurturance, sexuality and family. Any such form - whether it is open bonding, closed bonding, celibate bonding, serial bonding, one parent family, two parent family, multi-parent family, or any other - is chosen awarely in the presence of others, there is a support network for it, and there is an acknowledged social process for changing it.

9. We want to explore forms of conflict resolution: different ways of dealing with hostility and tension, irrational outbursts, irreconcilable opinions, broken agreements, confusion of purpose, and so on. We want to devise such forms, have them in readiness, and learn to use them when they are relevant.

10. We want to explore and improvise rituals, special events, holidays and feast-days, to celebrate, mark, or mourn the great recurring themes of individual, social and planetary life: birth, coming of age, relationships, graduations, visits, arrivals and departures, beginnings and endings, the seasons, solar and lunar cycles, death, and so on. We want to explore, receive and improvise rituals and other forms of inquiry: to foster our inward, occult and spiritual development; to interact with the subtle worlds, their powers and presences; and in communion together to attune to the life divine within and beyond, and present as, creation.

**We choose a realistic starting place.**

Since a self-generating culture, interweaving these many strands, cannot be achieved overnight, or indeed with any kind of improper haste, we choose to begin realistically where we are and with others who can commence in the same way.

Wherever we start, even if with only one strand, it is implicit at the outset that all the other strands are latent, and waiting their moment to come into expressive life, whether in this generation, the next, or in the generations to come.

# 3 Relational spirituality

A convincing account of spirituality for me is that it is about multi-faceted integral development explored by persons in relation. This is because many basic modes of human development - e.g. those to do with gender, psychosexuality, emotional and interpersonal skills, communicative competence, morality, to name but a few - unfold through engagement with other people. A person cannot develop these on their own, but through *mutual co-inquiry*. The spirituality that is the fullest development of these modes can only be achieved through relational forms of practice that unveil the spirituality implicit in them (Heron 1998; Perspectives 9 and 17 in this book)).

In short, the spirituality of persons is developed and revealed primarily in their relations with other persons. If you regard spirituality primarily as the fruit of individual practices, such as meditative attainment, then you can have the gross anomaly of a 'spiritual' person who is an interpersonal oppressor, and the possibility of 'spiritual' traditions that are oppression-prone (Heron, 1998; Kramer and Alstad, 1993; Trimondi and Trimondi, 2003). If you regard spirituality as centrally about liberating relations *between* people, then a new era of participative religion opens up, and this calls for a radical restructuring and reappraisal of traditional spiritual maps and routes.

Certainly there are important individualistic modes of development that do not necessarily directly involve engagement with other people, such as contemplative competence, and physical fitness. But these are secondary and supportive of those that do, and are in turn enhanced by co-inquiry with others.

On this overall view, spirituality is located in the interpersonal heart of the human condition where people co-operate to explore meaning, build relationship and manifest creativity through collaborative action inquiry into multi-modal integration and consummation. I propose one *possible* model of such collegial applied spirituality with at least eight distinguishing characteristics.

1. It is developmentally holistic, involving diverse major modes of human development; and the holism is both within each mode and as between the modes. Prime value is put on relational modes, such as gender, psychosexuality, emotional and interpersonal skills,

communicative competence, peer communion, peer decision-making, morality, human ecology, and more, supported by the individualistic, such as contemplative competence, physical fitness.

2. It is psychosomatically holistic, embracing a fully embodied and vitalized expression of spirit. Spirituality is found not just at the 'top end' of a developmental mode, but in the ground, the living root of its embodied form, in the relational heart of its current level of unfolding, and in the transcendent awareness embracing it.

3. It is epistemologically holistic, embracing many ways of knowing: knowing by presence with, by intuiting significant form and process, by conceptualizing, by practising. Such holistic knowing is intrinsically dialogic, action- and inquiry-oriented. It is fulfilled in peer-to-peer participative inquiry, and the participation is both epistemic and political.

4. It is ontologically holistic, open to the manifest as nature, culture and the subtle, and to spirit as immanent life, the situational present, and transcendent mind. It sees our social relations in this present situation – our process in this place - as the immediate locus of the unfolding integration of immanent and transcendent spirit (Heron, 1998, 2005, 2006).

5. It is focussed on worthwhile practical purposes that promote a flourishing humanity-cum-ecosystem; that is, it is rooted in an extended doctrine of rights with regard to social and ecological liberation.

6. It embraces peer-to-peer, participatory forms of decision-making. The latter in particular can be seen as a core discipline in relational spirituality, burning up a lot of the privatized ego. Participatory decision-making involves the integration of autonomy (deciding for oneself), co-operation (deciding with others) and hierarchy (deciding for others). As the bedrock of relational spirituality, I return to it at the end of the paper.

7. It honours the gradual emergence and development of peer-to-peer forms of association and practice, in every walk of life, in industry, in knowledge generation, in religion, and many more.

8. It affirms the role of both initiating hierarchy, and spontaneously surfacing and rotating hierarchy among the peers, in such emergence. More on this later on.

Once it is grasped that the spirituality of persons is developed and revealed primarily in the spirituality of their relations with other persons, that as such it is a form of participative peer-to-peer inquiry, and that all this is a new religious dawn, without historical precedent, then it is reasonable to suppose that any authentic development of human spirituality in the future can only emerge within the light of this dawn. In other words, if a form of spirituality is not co-created and co-authenticated by those who practise it, it involves some kind of indoctrination, and is therefore, in this day and age, of questionable worth.

## Spiritual leadership within an extended doctrine of rights

I prefer to think of the spiritual development of human culture as rooted in degrees of relational, moral insight and not in an evolutionary logic. Evolution as a concept seems best left to natural processes. Otherwise intellectual bids to know what *cultural* evolution is up to, rapidly convert into hegemonic arrogance and attempts at social and intellectual control. The developing of the human spirit in cultural forms is a different category and is very close in my view to the way in which our realization of an extended doctrine of rights, in theory and practice, can unfold.

There seem to be at least four degrees of such unfolding:

- Autocratic cultures which define rights in a limited and oppressive way and there are no rights of political participation.

- Narrow democratic cultures which practise political participation through representation, but have no or very limited participation of people in decision-making in all other realms, such as research, religion, education, industry, etc.

- Wider democratic cultures which practice both political participation and varying degrees of wider kinds of participation.

- Commons peer-to-peer cultures in a libertarian and abundance-oriented global network with equipotential rights of participation in decision-making of everyone in every field of human endeavour, *in relation to nature, culture, the subtle and the spiritual.*

These four degrees could be stated in terms of the relations between hierarchy, co-operation and autonomy (deciding for others, deciding with others, deciding by oneself).

- Hierarchy defines, controls and constrains co-operation and autonomy.

- Hierarchy empowers a measure of co-operation and autonomy in the political sphere only.

- Hierarchy empowers a measure of co-operation and autonomy in the political sphere and in varying degrees in other spheres.

- The sole role of hierarchy is in its spontaneous emergence in (a) the initiation, and (b) the continuous flowering, of autonomy-in-co-operation, of spirit-in-manifestation, in all spheres of human endeavour.

To elaborate this last point: creative leadership initiatives are taken by those who launch and empower co-operative groups of autonomous people. Charismatic empowering leadership of this kind is fundamental. Once the groups are up and running, charisma devolves and rotates: developmental initiatives are taken spontaneously by different peers at different times, and with respect to varying issues, in order further to enhance the flourishing of autonomy and co-operation within the group, within networks of groups, within the parity of spirit (Heron, 1997, 1998, 1999, 2006).

# 4 A dynamic participatory worldview

## A participatory worldview

In an article on 'A participatory inquiry paradigm' (Heron and Reason, 1997) the authors wrote that "experiential encounter with the presence of the world is the ground of our being and knowing" and that such encounter "articulates reality through inner resonance with what there is and through perceptually enacting its forms of appearing". My purpose in this Perspective is to explore these assertions in greater theological depth.

The world as I experience it is co-created by persons in participative relation with *what there is*: the sensory human shapes and is shaped by the given cosmos in a process of reciprocal encounter. This co-creating relation is the source and foundation of human languages, which may either reveal or obscure it. And within this prelinguistic relation, *what there is* manifests as "presences in communion with other presences, in a great field of mutual participation" (Heron, 1996a: 192). In using everyday language we name such presences as persons, plants, animals, stones, earth, energies, entities, etc., and as the spaces and places these beings generate in and through their mutual engagement.

## The divine as the relation of co-creation

I define the divine, initially, as the experiential relation of mutual participation and co-creation between presences. For us as persons, the divine is the here and now intimacy of this relation, constituted by and inclusive of the immediate field of participating presences. This explicit experiential field has a graduated edge of transcendent infinite horizons, an implicitly limitless field of further participating presences with which we tacitly engage. The explicit experiential field also has an immanent infinitude within: the unfathomable inwardness and interiority, the illimitable internal source, of each and all participating presences. The co-creating relation within our immediate experiential field of participating presences, within the aegis of these complementary infinitudes, is what I name the divine. This provides a more precise account of Karl Rahner's notion of 'unthematic experience', which in his theology is the inherent openness of the human prior to all education, to the infinite divine (Kelly, 1993).

Is the divine One or Many? It is One-Many: the relation of mutual participation and co-creation is unitive; at the same time, the presences thus related are multiple. The unitive relation of mutual co-creation includes its diversity of presences and of forms of co-creation. The multiplicity of presences presupposes the unitive relation which co-creates their manifest forms.

## Co-presencing and co-enacting

The relation of mutual co-creation between presences is both a co-presencing and a co-enacting. Through co-presencing - mutual resonance and attunement, reciprocal participative empathy - we enter into each other and affirm our unity at the same time as affirming ourselves as beings with unique kinds of inwardness: we co-create both our togetherness and our distinctness. Through co-enactment - mutual perceiving - we give form to our respective kinds of spatiotemporal appearance: through sensory and more-than-sensory kinds of interactive construing and constructing, we co-create a conscious world of life, motion, and form within which we time and space our own distinct gestures of being in a choreographic relation with each other.

On this view the notions of both empathy and perception undergo an enlargement of meaning. If a person engages with a rock, they co-presence each other, that is, reciprocally resonate and empathize. The rock in its own way attunes to and affirms the presence of person, just as the person does in a distinctive way with the presence of the rock. And they co-enact each other, mutually perceive and construe each other. The rock as an energy system constructs a form of the appearing person just as the person uniquely images the appearance of the rock in tactile, visual and auditory form. The relation is mutual, grounded in the meeting and engagement of differences.

Empathy and perception as universal processes are combined in Whitehead's notion of prehension, a reciprocal taking account, by dynamic events of all kinds, of each other's energetic processes and their concomitant emotional tone (Whitehead, 1926). He quotes with approval the famous passage from Francis Bacon in *Silva Silvarum*: "It is certain that all bodies whatsoever, though they have no sense, yet they have perception: for when one body is applied to another, there is a kind of election to embrace that which is agreeable, and to exclude or expel that which is ingrate; and whether the body be alterant or altered, evermore a perception precedeth operation; for else all bodies would be alike one to another."

Abram, following Merleau-Ponty (1962), affirms our ongoing reciprocity with the world, prior to all our verbal reflections. At the preconceptual level, our spontaneous sensorial engagement with phenomena is an experience of reciprocal encounter with dynamic presences that draw us into relation. To touch is to feel oneself being touched, to see is to feel oneself seen. The surroundings are experienced as sensate, attentive and watchful (Abram, 1996: 53-72).

### Practising the presence of the divine

To practise the presence of the divine is to open ourselves to our ever-present co-creating relation with other presences, a relation that is continuously active within our immediate experiential field. There are certain relations within this field that are closely interdependent and always active. They are the dynamic relation of our being:

- With the presence of air in our breathing

- With the presence of the ground in our standing

- With the presence of place - and its constitutive presences - in our time-space gestures of sound or silence, of movement or posture

- With the presence of the sky and horizon in our vision.

These co-creating relations are distinct here and now epiphanies within the embrace of transcendent horizons and immanent depths. And we can take them awarely into dynamic relation with other persons in a co-creating field, in which each person interacts with every other through intentional, spontaneous moving and sounding. This is a relational dance of the kinaesthetic, the motile, the tactile, the auditory, the visual and the vocal in mutual participation and exchange. It gives the fullest, most explicit, account of participative, co-creating relations within the immediate conditions of human embodiment. Thus, in our mutual presencing and imaginal engagement, in terms of our basic epiphanies, we as humans practise in a special way the relational presence of the divine. Such interactive presencing overflows into, is consummated by and manifested in, daily forms of living - in familial, institutional, economic and ecological transformative activity.

### Sacred science

This kind of sacred collaborative practice of the presence of the divine is also an incipient co-operative inquiry into it. The sacred inquiry is conducted in terms of a dynamic interplay between experiential knowing, presentational knowing, propositional knowing and practical knowing:

- The experiential knowing is of our co-creating relation with other presences and with each other in the immediate here and now field.

- The presentational knowing is in symbolizing this experiential knowing in patterns of interactive sound and movement.

- The propositional knowing is present as critical subjectivity, a vigilant discrimination that monitors what is going on in the light of critical standards and keeps it free of emotional distortion.

The practical knowing, the knowing how, is twofold:

- The skill in the expressive, symbolizing use of interactive sound and movement.

- The very subtle skill in managing congruence between the four forms of knowing, so that no one of them takes off on its own alienated from the other two.

The fundamental research cycling is the continuous interplay between the four kinds of knowing. This is religious action inquiry for each individual and an incipient co-operative inquiry for the group as a whole. The inquiry entails skilled action (practical knowing), monitored by vigilant discrimination (propositional knowing), that symbolizes (presentational knowing) our co-creating relations with other presences and each other (experiential knowing). In such inquiry, the element of celebration, of ecstatic abundance, evident in skilled presentational expression is prior to, is wider and deeper than, the element of inquiry its symbolism embraces.

The research cycling becomes more complete, and the co-operative inquiry more overt, when it is extended to include phases of explicit conceptual reflection. There is a great deal of virtue in delaying this phase for a long while. This is partly because in our culture it is very easy for such reflection to become rapidly dissociated from its relevant experiential base, and thus to disregard, denigrate or deny it. It is also because the interplay of the four kinds of knowing in the interactive religious inquiry needs a substantial period of ripening and maturity before it can provide a stable foundation for systematic reflection.

**Motion, mysticism and magic**

Human beings in active relation with each other, in their breathing, in their grounding, in their time-space sounding and movement, in their vision, in the context of immanent and transcendent infinitudes - all this is a practice of the presence of the divine which honour the fullness of human expressiveness and participative engagement. It presupposes:

- Body-mind integration: dealing with repression, emotional competence, charismatic disinhibition - a trio of related processes.

- Interpersonal integration: dealing with projections, authentic interaction (openness, honesty, congruence), resonant attunement - a related trio of related processes.

- Group-planet integration: dealing with ecoblindness, holonomic awareness (this place as a coded form of the whole planet), responsiveness to the presence and presences of place - a third trio of related processes.

# 5 Sacred science defined

The purpose of this Perspective is to propose some basic defining features of a sacred science. Sacred science presupposes a view of the sacred and of science. The account it gives of science further presupposes a paradigm of inquiry, a set of views about reality, about knowing, and about values - an ontology, epistemology, and axiology - metaphysical views which determine the format of the methodology used. Scientific method does not establish a view of reality, it gives systematic expression to a preconceived view.

**The sacred**

The sacred I define as:

- The all-inclusive illimitable presence of *what there is*.

- That which calls human beings to comprehensive flourishing in relation with *what there is*.

The holy calls to active wholeness in every respect. Active wholeness manifests holiness: it is an epiphany of the sacred.

**Science**

I define science as an activity which exercises critical rigour in articulating human experience of what there is. These are the twin pillars of the scientific enterprise: discriminating judgment and being engaged with what is going on. Each of these has two sets of correlative aspects or poles.

Discriminating judgment is individual and collective. It involves:

- Personal apprehension and reflection.

- Shared debate and dialogue.

Discriminating judgment also has two correlative kinds of process:

- Apprehending the significance of patterns.

- Understanding the validity of propositions.

Being engaged with what there is has a subjective and an objective component. The process is:

- In terms of our own sensitivities.

- And it relates to what is there, to what is cosmically given.

Being engaged with what there is also has two correlative processes:

- Meeting what there is.

- Taking action in relation to what there is

## Ontology: a view of present reality

Implicit in this account of science is a view of present reality. Present reality is not the same as what there is, as the cosmically given. It is what-there-is as we encounter it, as we come to know it through embodiment-in-our-world. This grounding, present reality of the scientific enterprise has the following properties:

*Present reality is subjective-objective.* More fully stated, reality is subjective-intersubjective-objective. In the very process of meeting what there is, we know there is a cosmic given, which at the same time is given shape by our enacting it, our framing and forming it, in terms of our own sensitivities - including perceiving, imaging and feeling - and cultural belief systems. Reciprocally, what there is shapes our shaping of it. There are two further ways of stating this point:

- *Present reality is mediate-immediate.* It is mediated in terms of our own sensitivities and beliefs. It is immediate because we touch, meet, encounter, engage with, what there is.

- *Present reality is relative-universal.* It is relative to our mediation of it within our context. It is universal because of our immediate touch with what there is.

*Present reality is participative.* In framing what there is, our sensitivities partake of it, share in it, enter into it, are conjoined with it, indwell it. Reciprocally, in the process of shaping our framing, the given indwells it.

*Present reality is incomplete.* The degree of participation between subject and object, the knower and the known, perceiver and perceived, the receiver and the given, is partial. It is transient, perspectival, contextually relative, changing, capable of expansion and contraction.

*Present reality is distinctive.* Subject and object, knower and known, perceiver and perceived transcend their transient and partial relation of mutual participation. Such transcendence, or unmanifest potential, is evident as the distinctness of each.

*Present reality is seamless.* There is no gap between subject and object, knower and known. The subjective-objective relation of participation is seamless, without separation. It is a relation of nonseparable distinctness within partial union.

*Present reality is multi-levelled.* It includes an interconnected set of distinct subjective-objective worlds, articulated by the range of human sensitivities from the obvious to the subtle.

## Epistemology: an account of ways of knowing

On the view presented in this book, sacred science involves four forms of knowing which are mutually supportive and correlative with each other. Henceforth, I shall use the single term 'being' as synonymous with 'what there is' and 'the cosmically given'.

*Sacred science is practical.* It is engaged with the active transformation of the human experience of being, in the interests of comprehensive flourishing, individual, social, natural, subtle and cosmic. Transformative know-how, skill, I call *practical knowing*.

*Sacred science is conceptual.* It is committed to use language to generate conceptual models and maps which symbolize the human experience of being; and to apply to these models rational canons of internal consistency and coherence with experience. This is *propositional knowing*.

*Sacred science is aesthetic.* It seeks to symbolize and evoke the human experience of being through non-discursive expressive forms, that is, in terms of visual, auditory and kinaesthetic patterns which exhibit aesthetic canons of vital and formal significance. Such expressive significance I call *presentational knowing*.

*Sacred science is empirical.* It is based on an appeal to human experience of being - in social, natural and subtle worlds, in their cosmic setting and ground. Such experience is inclusive of the whole range of sensitivities whereby human beings engage with other humans, other life forms, physical and subtle worlds, their wider universe and their ground. This unrestricted engagement I call *experiential knowing*.

There are other key concepts which deal with the relation between these four forms of knowing, in particular their congruence. There are two kinds of congruence:

- *Groundedness.* Forms of knowing lower down in the above list are the epistemological ground, the validating foundation of those higher up.

- *Consummation.* Forms of knowing higher up consummate and fulfil at a new level of relative autonomy those lower down.

Thus we have complementary interacting forms of congruence such that experiential knowing is the foundation of the three forms of knowing which progressively consummate it, and practical knowing is the consummation of the three forms of knowing which successively support it. These complementary forms of congruence expand into another important relation:

- *The cycle of accumulative flourishing.* Practical knowing, when it involves transformative action and skill, leads over into new experiential encounter, richer and deeper forms of experiential knowing. Thus transformative practical knowing, which is grounded on, and consummates at a new level of relative autonomy, current experiential knowing, leads over into enriched experiential knowing which is the ground of more deeply transformative practical knowing, and so on.

## Axiology: a view on value

Sacred science presupposes a view that what is intrinsically valuable - an end in itself, worthwhile simply by virtue of its own inherent nature - is comprehensive human flourishing in relation with being. This value is the call, the beckoning of the sacred: to become whole, hale, holy. We articulate our relationship with being in two sets of bipolar correlates: (1) our individual and our social life; (2) our planetary and our cosmic context. With regard to each of these there is a political dimension and an epistemic dimension: the former both consummates and is grounded on the latter.

*Political flourishing in individual and social life.* I conceive such flourishing as a process of social participation in which there is a mutually enabling balance between autonomy, co-operation and hierarchy; and which is interdependent with the flourishing of the planetary ecosystem.

- By autonomy I mean a state of being in which each person can in liberty determine and fulfil their own true needs and interests. I do not here mean the autonomy of the isolated and dissociated Cartesian ego, but the autonomy of the person in a deeply participative relationship with being and other beings.
- By co-operation I mean mutual aid and support between autonomous persons, including participative decision-making, negotiation and conflict resolution. Participative decision-making enables peo-

ple to be involved in the making of decisions, in every social context, which affect their flourishing in any way; and through which people also speak on behalf of the wider ecosystem of which they are part.

- By hierarchy I mean a state of being in which a person appropriately takes temporary responsibility for doing things to or for other persons for the sake of their future autonomy and co-operation. This is part of parenthood, education and many professions.

This is a dynamic account of intrinsic value: to do with the politics of choice and action. Autonomy is about deciding for oneself, co-operation about deciding with others, and hierarchy about deciding for others. And this order seems to be paramount. Only persons who know what their own preferences are can negotiate and co-operate effectively in conjoint decisions. People who do not really know where they stand on an issue have no proper ground for co-operation, and can only huddle together in the middle of a fudge.

Even more critically, a person who does not know how to be autonomous and co-operative cannot make effective decisions for other people to empower their future autonomy and co-operation. Leaders who are not inwardly free can only lead people into sustained submission and subpersonhood. So hierarchy has human value when:

- It is manifested by a person well-grounded in their own autonomy and co-operation, both rooted in a deeply participative relationship with being and other beings.

- It is exercised to empower the emergence of autonomy and co-operation in others.

- It is reduced as that emergence occurs.

- It is abandoned when that emergence has occurred; otherwise it is disvaluable and oppressive of human emergence. [For issues of hierarchies of the second and third kind, and of two-world politics, see Heron (2006)].

*Epistemic flourishing in individual and social life.* This involves a growing participative awareness of social contexts, from face-to-face interactions, through local, regional, national and federal to global associations of people. It means a conscious indwelling, and resonance with, the cultural life of our planet in its many aspects from the small to the large scale. There is also the issue of awareness of what is going on in related unseen dimensions of being, in interpenetrating subtle realms.

*Political flourishing in our planetary and cosmic context.* I conceive such flourishing as a process of ecoparticipation. This is political participation of humans in and with their nonhuman environment in its fullest sense, local, global, cosmic, and on interrelated levels of present reality. It means making decisions in managing our environment in all its aspects to enhance the well-being of diversity, communion and encompassing holarchy.

*Epistemic flourishing in our planetary and cosmic context.* This involves a growing participative awareness of, felt resonance with, the physiosphere, the biosphere, the solar system and the galaxy, and their subtle correlates.

## Methodology: an account of how to inquire

The foundation, the ground, of sacred science is experiential knowing. It ultimately appeals to unrestricted human experience of being, which is inclusive of the whole range of sensitivities whereby embodied persons engage with other persons, other life forms, physical and subtle worlds, their wider universe and their ground. The consummation of sacred science is practical knowing: the active transformation of the human experience of being, in the interests of comprehensive flourishing, individual and social, planetary and cosmic. Presentational and propositional knowing mediate between these two poles. Weaving these four forms into inquiry method means:

*Research cycling for congruence.* The inquiry cycles through the four forms of knowing to enhance their congruence, both as groundedness and as consummation. In basic terms, the cycles move to an fro between phases of discriminating judgment and phases of engagement with what there is. Such intentional and aware research cycling is a way of promoting critical subjectivity and critical intersubjectivity.

- *The discriminating judgment phase.* This involves presentational and propositional knowing: data-sharing, sense-making, review and reflection on past engagement, and forward planning for future engagement.

- *The engagement phase.* This involves practical and experiential knowing: taking action in relation to what there is and attuning to it.

*Primacy of the practical.* Because the sacred calls human beings to comprehensive flourishing in relation to what there is, the primary intended outcome of sacred science is practical knowing, the active transformation of the human experience of being. The main goal, end, purpose of the inquiry is transformational competence - the skill, the know-how involved in active flourishing in relation with being. This is, of course, inseparable from outcomes in terms of experiential knowing - felt encounter with what there is.

*Autonomous inquiry.* This is the foundation method of sacred science. Without a genuine autonomous inquiry, in which the individual explores his or her own relationship with being, there can be no basis for an authentic co-operative inquiry. This exploration includes individual discriminating judgment, that is, critical subjectivity.

*Co-operative inquiry.* This is the central method of sacred science. Two or more persons co-operate in choosing the focus of inquiry, and in designing how they will explore it through experience and action. They then engage in the action phase, after which they collaborate in reviewing it, refining their account of the focus, and in the light of this plan the next action phase. And so on. The core of the reflection phase is peer discrimination, that is, critical intersubjectivity (Heron, 1996a, 1998; Heron and Reason, 2001).

*Hierarchical inquiry.* The hierarchical principle is manifest in two ways; first, in the initiation of the inquiry by one or two persons; and second, in spontaneous rotation among the inquiring peers, as one or another member has an insight which illuminates and advances the peer decision-making process.

*Validity procedures.* There are a whole range of procedures for looking into the soundness of the inquiry process. They include: the balance between divergence and convergence in research cycling; authentic collaboration; challenging consensus collusion; managing distress; balancing reflection and action; attending to the dynamic between chaos and order (Heron, 1996a).

**Autonomous practice**

I end this Perspective with a brief hierarchical, initiating suggestion about sacred science practices for the individual, autonomous inquirer. I will address the description of their format directly to you, the reader. They are all about an active transformation of your human experience of being, in the interests of comprehensive flourishing. They are grounded in my own autonomous inquiry, and are not vested with any external authority. They may or may not speak to your condition. They may need reframing to ignite your attention and interest. They may be constitutionally irrelevant. They may be just what you need at this time.

*Attend to your perceiving a world.* Note that there is no gap between your attention and your imaging - seeing, hearing, touching - and what is there. It is a seamless experiential whole.

*Attend to your own potential.* Feel into what you can become, your potential for transformation. Note that it is a well-spring from an infinitude within.

*Attend to your attention and turn about within it.* Note that it is continuous with a vast backdrop of oceanic awareness.

*Attend to your attention and look upwards within it.* Note that it is a ray of awareness emanating ecstatically from above.

# 6 Theology basics

The participatory fruits of spiritual inquiry explored in this and the next several Perspectives are personal fruits. They are my conceptual distinctions, a set of working principles, and further develop the theological sketch in Perspective 4. They are grounded in three kinds of inquiry which are interdependent and mutually involved in each other:

- They are co-created in a personal participatory relation with being, a relation which is rooted in the human capacity for feeling the presence of what there is. This radical capacity I explore in depth in *Feeling and Personhood* (Heron, 1992). Ferrer gives a related account of participatory knowing as presential, enactive and transformative (Ferrer, 2002: 122-3).

- They are generated in a context of a variety of collaborative spiritual inquiries, including an ongoing relationship inquiry, a current long-term co-operative inquiry now (2006) into its twelfth year, and over twenty short-term co-operative inquiries since 1978 - several of which are reported in *Sacred Science* (Heron, 1998).

- They are influenced by acquaintance with, reflection on, and discussions within, the wider personal, cultural and historical context, including the great legacy of religious beliefs and experiential data from spiritual schools ancient and modern, western and eastern.

These three kinds of inquiry provide a qualified warrant for my text. On the one hand it present ideas that are clarified and critically refined in personal and interpersonal enactments of what there is, and are thus one modestly valid perspective on, and revelation of, the mystery of being. On the other hand they are relative to the cultural and historical contexts within which they are framed, and thus are fallible and nonperennial, an invitation to dialogue and further inquiry.

To say that a theological vision is co-created in a personal and an interpersonal participative relation with being, and in the qualifying contexts stated, means neither that it is universally absolute, nor that it is an entirely relativistic construction. It means that it is one relative perspective brought forth *with* what is universal, and calls for other diverse perspectives, grounded in inquiry, to honour the fullness of the mystery.

I will make a few points here about the role of past spiritual traditions in making contemporary spiritual distinctions:

- They have an important secondary and contributory role, via their massive heritage of spiritual lore. This lore is the indispensable loam which nourishes present growth. However, the primary role is for the contemporary voice of innovative divine becoming, surfacing now through the constraints of what is today outmoded in this great inheritance from the aspirations of our forbears.

- The idea that there is a perennial (lasting-forever) philosophy which can be extracted from past religions and which lays down the basic structure of spiritual practice far off into the distant future, seems to me as fanciful as the idea of a perennial natural science. To restrict postmodern spirituality by principles derived from premodern spirituality is like constraining the future of chemistry by the precepts of alchemy. Perennial philosophy prescriptions strike me as a rearguard action to defend established centres of spiritual authority from having to deal with radical change. See *Sacred Science* (Heron, 1998: 43-46).

- Past belief-systems and practices reflect past contexts. Current contexts call both for respect for past traditions and for a radical revisionary overhaul of some of their most fundamental beliefs, attitudes and behaviours.

So in the spirit of both respect and revision, I distinguish in what follows between the divine, the manifest and the spiritual; and between three forms of the manifest, and three forms of the spiritual. It is important to note that these conceptual distinctions are at one and the same time the *fruits of inquiry*, *possible guidelines for inquiry* and above all are *subject to further inquiry* - of the three kinds mentioned at the outset.

**The divine**

The *presence* of the totality of what there is in every respect without let or hindrance. An integral Many-One reality including the **manifest** and the **spiritual** in all their modes.

Note here that the spiritual is included in, but not identical with, the divine, which is a more comprehensive reality. To regard spirit as identical with the divine leads to acosmic monism: the reduction of the Many to the One, and of the manifest to the spiritual. It also fosters spiritual practices which flee to god from the works of god, individual inflation rather than relational engagement, and a strong element of misogyny.

## The manifest

The diverse realms and entities of creation, in two known primary forms.

### The phenomenal

Human beings in our world, which includes the physical cosmos, the biological, psychological and cultural spheres. The human and physical sciences, comprehensively considered, are fields of inquiry which constitute just one half of inquiry into the manifest. I use 'phenomenal' here with the meaning of 'known through the senses'.

### The subtle

Energies, domains, presences and powers to which extrasensory capacities in humans bear witness. The subtle appears to permeate and sustain the phenomenal realm, and also to reach far beyond it. It has often been called the psychical, as in the field of psychical research.

The subtle realms, in all their majesty and vastness, have been by various constituencies: dismissed as non-existent; or subjectivized - that is, regarded as purely psychological in character; or castigated as distractions on the way to the Absolute; or regarded as projected forms of what is as yet unrealized in the higher Self; or feared as the work of the devil; or simply left out of account. I don't believe that any of these views will really do. They avoid the challenge of systematic inquiry into what is probably the greater part of divine creation. This inquiry is the other half of inquiry into the manifest.

### The intermediate

The zone of interaction of the phenomenal and the subtle. There are two hypothetical aspects of this zone:

- *The archnatural:* the subtle as the formative matrix of the phenomenal, as the active intermediary between the spiritual and the phenomenal.

- *The psychoid:* the subtle effects of human intentionality in the phenomenal realm.

Both of these are important hypotheses, and their potential implications for how we live on this planet call for radical inquiry.

## The spiritual

An all-pervasive conscious animation informing the manifest, both phenomenal and subtle. It has three known primary aspects:

### The situational

The living spirit of our present situation, our current process in the world, our immediate engagement with what there is, in its three inter-related aspects, the third being the ground of the other two. We can open to it as:

- The presence of location, of a particular place and time, of being here now.

- The spirit of occasion: a birth, a death, a greeting, a meeting, an occupational task, making love, a ritual of celebration, and a myriad other events.

- The reality of relationship, Shekinah, the Between, the spirit that connects,; the *distinctness-in-unity* of subject and object, subject and subject, as we participate in our multidimensional world, perceiving and engaging with nature, culture and other realms.

Compare Jorge Ferrer's important notion of transpersonal phenomena not as individual inner experiences, but as events in reality in which our consciousness creatively participates. These include I-Thou relationships, communal spiritual occasions, collective identities such as archetypal morphic fields, sacred places, communion with nature (Ferrer, 2002). An influential precursor here is Martin Buber (1937), who proposed a shift from an individual to a dialogical and relational concept of spirituality, and affirmed the spiritual realm of the Between as establishing authentic community.

For a simple opening to situational spirit in relation to the immediate physical environment, try the following. Stand in front of a kitchen workbench, or a surface of similar height so that you can touch it without having to stoop. Place your hands palms flat upon the surface and look out at the world through the window. Let go of egoic contraction by expanding into the space behind the eyes, and behind the spine. Then let your awareness fall into the great open space behind and below you, as you participate in being-in-a-world through posture, touch, seeing and hearing. With this simple magic you find the wrap-around of inner and outer, of awareness and its contents, all one with multifarious distinctions. For another account of the same process, and for interpersonal versions, see *Seamless perceiving* in Perspective 9 below.

*The immanent*

The spiritual life-potential embedded within creation, the indwelling source of manifest becoming, the drive of emergent development. We can open to it as:

- The motivation of cosmic unfolding, including the dynamic ground of our will to live both as an individual and as a universal citizen of cosmopolis.

- The creative cosmic womb, including the spiritual womb within our embodiment, whence emerge our potentials and creative innovations.

- The pregnant void that is the mystery of spirit within the manifest.

Note that 'immanent' has traditionally been used, in ambiguous and confusing ways, to refer to spirit both as 'the situational' and 'the immanent' in my terms.

For the spirit as ground, compare Schelling's *deus implicitus*, more recently reappearing as the "Dynamic Ground (libido, psychic energy, numinous power or spirit) of somatic, instinctual, affective and creative-imaginal potentials" (Washburn, 1995); the "Entelechy Self...the Root Self, the ground of one's being, and the seeded coded essence in you which contains both the patterns and the possibilities of your life" (Houston, 1987); of "Eros as spirit-in-action", the indwelling divine drive at the root of human aspiration (Wilber, 1995).

*The transcendent*

Cosmic consciousness which is beyond and encompassing creation, and is the origin of its formative archetypes. We can participate in this consciousness in its several aspects as :

- The sustaining, managerial intelligence of the universe.

- The Logos, creative divine speech which utters the universe.

- Indeterminate ineffability, beyond all name and form.

Here we celebrate the great legacy of the mysticism of transcendence which we inherit from diverse traditions over the past three thousand years. For an overview of historical precursors to these aspects of the transcendent see *Sacred Science* (Heron, 1998: 89-90).

The three aspects of spirit as portrayed in this section - the situational, the immanent, the transcendent – honour both traditional and contemporary accounts of human experience of the divine. And the assertions made in this Perspective about them call to be questioned within the practical inquiries described in Perspectives 9, 10 and 11.

Here is a diagrammatic summary of the main distinctions made in this Perspective:

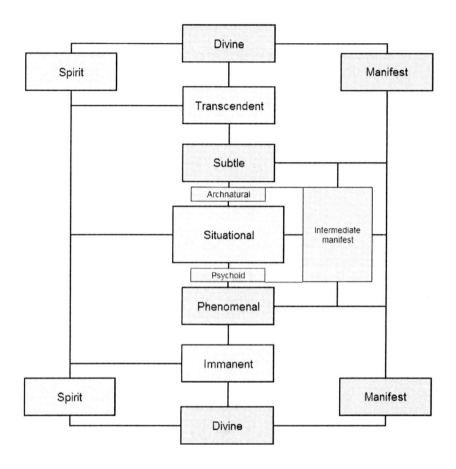

*Figure 1: main distinctions*

## The validation of spiritual insights

How do we assess the validity of this or any other insight into what is spiritually ultimate? How do we make qualitative distinctions among different enactions of the nature of the divine? This is a contentious area of discussion because it is not clear to me how anyone can re-spond to the question without simply turning their own enaction into a set of criteria for evaluating others. A more modest question is about the criteria I use to clarify the personal validity of my spiritual beliefs. Here are the basic ones:

- They affirm autonomous spirituality: authority resides in the internal monitor.

- They affirm relational spirituality: the central locus of the spiritual is between persons and between persons and their worlds.

- They affirm embodied spirituality: the primary energies of our embodiment reveal living spirit.

- They affirm transcendent spirituality: everyday awareness is continuous with a vast backdrop of universal consciousness.

Beyond this, the basic question is about *how I dialogue fruitfully* with persons who have criteria of validity different from my own.

# 7 Divine polarities

Let's now enact a hypothetical vision of some fundamental polarities in this divine scheme of things. By a polarity I mean two complementary principles - basic creative forms of dynamic distinctness-in-unity - which are interdependent and interact within the divine. And for us, where they interact is always in this situation, where we are in our universe.

The contemplation of these polarities helps me in the transition from the classical monopolar transcendent account of the spiritual which has dominated our planet for the past three thousand years, to a contemporary account of bipolar transcendent-immanent spirit mediated by the situational.

### The manifest and the spiritual

The fundamental polarity within the divine, analogous to the human body-mind.

### The phenomenal and the subtle

Complementary kinds of manifestation; polar forms of the experiential manifest body of the spiritual.

### The immanent and the transcendent

The complementarity within the spiritual, the polarity of indwelling emergent life-potential and transcendent archetypal consciousness. This polarity is mediated by situational spirit – the living presence of every situation where we are.

- *Situational spirit as dynamic mediator.* For us incarnate humans, spirit is first and foremost a presence in which we participate here where we are in this current situation, in our locality and social context in the universe. Here and now we are in a spirit-enfolded location. We are in the presence-between in our place. Awakening to this reality, opening to, and acting with, situational spirit is a dynamic integration of emergent life-potential, and emanating transcendent consciousness. I develop this theme later on.

- *Autonomy, hierarchy and co-operation.* A key aspect of this dynamic integration in human affairs is the interweaving of autonomy, hierarchy and co-operation. Emergent life-potential is the source of influence from the grass roots, from below upwards: it is the ground of autonomy, deciding for oneself. Transcendent consciousness is the guiding light of hierarchy, deciding for others. Situational spirit is the arena of human co-operation, deciding with others, which in a special way integrates both autonomy and hierarchy – more on this later. By the term 'hierarchy' on its own, here and elsewhere, I mean a down-hierarchy: see *Parity* below.

## The many and the one

There is one divine including the phenomenal cosmos, the subtle cosmos and spirit in its three modes. Within each kind of cosmos there are many forms and processes, and within spirit there are many distinct spiritual presences, including the human person. The distinctness of the many, both manifest and spiritual, is interdependent with the unity of the one. Distinctness is not separateness: distinctness celebrates diversity in free unity; separateness is a mental state of closure against unity.

## Becoming and being; the innovative and the conservative

The divine includes a process of becoming, of innovative change and development, and in the phenomenal realm human-divine interaction, in our situation here and now, is on the crest of such becoming. Complementary to this are divine constants, the conservative parameters of being which provide the context for innovative becoming and may be progressively modified by it.

## Centre and circumference

All actual entities in the process of situational becoming are poised between the emergence of their indwelling potential from their divine centre, and the transcendent encompassing calling of their archetype from their divine circumference.

## Autonomy and connectedness

All actual entities combine relatively independent functioning, and participatory engagement with other entities. This complementarity of autonomy in connectedness, when fully developed in humans, is what I call *collegiality* - diversity in free unity. Collegiality is rooted in dynamic spirit-enhancing mutual regard, the full flower of human living and loving.

## Polarity properties

Here are some key features which I find fruitful to enact with regard to these polarities, and I sketch out a few of their applications.

*Irreducibility*

The poles are both interdependent and irreducible to each other (Baum, 1953). Neither alone is sufficient and both are necessary. The mystery of the divine is that it defies reduction of either of its dynamic poles to the other. So creation cannot be regarded as the exclusive product either of descending emanation from the transcendent, as in the neo-Platonic doctrine of the great chain of being; or of ascending emergence from some amorphous primordial state. It is the co-product of a continuous interaction of emergence from the immanent depths, and emanation from the transcendent heights.

The manifest, I suggest, is not simply the product of a self-limiting process of the spiritual, as in the ancient Hindu view. An alternative approach is that the manifest and the spiritual are interdependent aspects of the divine: they are in different respects both dependent on, and independent of, each other. The traditional monism of absolute spirit denies the full interdependence of the manifest and the spiritual, insisting they are nondual in a way that essentially reduces the manifest to the spiritual, form to emptiness, fullness to the void.

A more radical kind of monism affirms the divine as the one ultimate being embracing the irreducible interdependent poles of the manifest and the spiritual, and proposes that they are diune. The traditional view tends to promote the liberation of souls from the manifest; the contemporary radical view calls for the liberation of persons in a just and flourishing society within the manifest. The diune is a developing realization, a situational unfolding; the nondual is an end-state of realization. Conceptually and intentionally, it is more liberating, fruitful and world-transformative to speak of two-in-one than not-two.

*Parity*

The word 'hierarchy' derives from two Greek words meaning 'sacred' and 'rule'. I prefer to talk about sacred influence rather than sacred rule. Sacred influence operates in two directions: up and down. The sacred influence of an up-hierarchy emerges from indwelling life-potential. Power is exercised in the direction of ascent. The seed is potent in relation to the impacted soil above it, breaking it up and pushing through it.

The sacred influence of a down-hierarchy emanates from transcendent consciousness. Power descends from what is over to what is under. Sunlight is potent in relation to the leafy branches below it.

The immanent and the transcendent, up-hierarchy and down-hierarchy, are of different natures that have equal status, are in a relation of parity within each actual situation where they interact. The sacred influence of Eros and the sacred influence of Logos are situationally equipotent, in a divine marriage of equals. They interact with reciprocal effect, neither dominant under or over the other. They are polar complements equally vital in the ordering of manifest situations.

On this view, parity is more fundamental in the scheme of things than hierarchy, for neither an up-hierarchy nor a down-hierarchy is properly exercised or understood save in a reciprocal peer relation with its complement.

So too, the manifest and the spiritual are of different natures that have equal status and value; and within the manifest, the phenomenal and the subtle. As complementary polar forms of the divine, and within the divine, these theological consorts call for equal honouring and celebration of their distinctive qualities.

The re-evaluation of these and the other polar consorts in terms of radical and thoroughgoing parity stands in marked contrast with traditional evaluations. Compare also the views of Victor and Victoria Trimondi on the creative polarity beyond Tantrism to be found on their website at *www.trimondi.de/SDLE/Postscript.htm.*

*Asymmetry*

The relation between the poles is asymmetrical. And there is a polarity within this asymmetry. One pole creatively fulfils and consummates the other, which is a ground and context of meaning for the first. I use here limited metaphorical approximations for a complementary dynamic within the divine. Thus the manifest creatively fulfils the spiritual and the spiritual provides a context of meaning for the manifest; the phenomenal creatively fulfils the subtle and the subtle provides a context of meaning for the phenomenal; the immanent creatively fulfils the transcendent and the transcendent provides a context of meaning for the immanent. So the divine poles declare their interdependence, irreducibility, parity of status, differential natures, and asymmetrical relations.

*Concentricity*

A simple diagram of concentric circles can symbolize the divine (Figure 2). The centre point represents spirit as the infinitude within, an immanent life, which moves everything with indwelling potential. An outermost circle represents spirit as the infinitude beyond, a transcendent consciousness, which emanates, and informs and calls everything with the archetypes of creation. An inner circle around the centre represents the phenomenal, and another circle between this and the outermost circle represents the subtle, both interfused with spirit as situational. All these four together symbolize the divine. The phenomenal circle of human experience is open to situational spirit here and now – symbolized by the space around the circle - and beyond this can open to the circumference and to the centre, in qualitatively different dipolar practices, as described in a later Perspective.

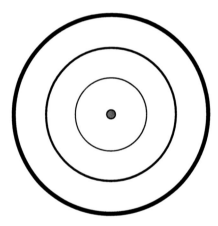

*Figure 2: the divine*

**Human mediation**

From our human point of view, the only place where the divine poles interact and influence us, and whence they are accessible, is in our current situation, our here and now locality in our universe. We, in how we are being and doing in our present place, are the integrating mediators of fundamental polar parameters of the divine. Situational spirit is the ever-developing and unfolding human-divine co-creation of this integration. In this matter, we are theurgists, changing the nature of the divine in collaborative transactions with the divine. Or, if you prefer to put it theocentrically, the divine innovates through manifesting as imaginative co-creative humans. See Figure 3.

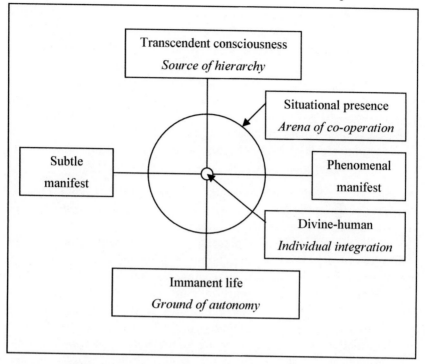

*Figure 3: divine-human integration*

All the following parameters of the human condition call to be involved and awarely re-evaluated in our mediating role.

- The human situation is an embodied situation. We are rooted in the several primary energies/drives of our bodily endowment, and in the particular place in which we choose to live upon our planet. These primary energies and our location are grounded in, and basic openings to, the divine.

- The human situation is also a 'we' situation, inherently intersubjective and social. For each of us it is moulded both in belief and in action by how we use a shared language in dialogue with others, and by how we selectively interpret, in relationship with others, the values, norms, and beliefs of our culture which that language mediates. All this shapes our shaping of the divine.

- Persons become persons in and through relationship with other persons. Autonomy flourishes in creative kinds of connectedness with other autonomous people. Full and profound participation in embodied divinity is through the collegiality of fully embodied co-inquirers: people discussing options and deciding actions to transform their personhood, their society and their planet. In this practice, each person moves between and integrates three positions: autonomy - being clear what I genuinely need, want and wish for, what my idiosyncratic preferences are, in relation to the matter being discussed; hierarchy - thinking on behalf of the whole group and the wider community within which the action will be embedded; and co-operation - listening to, empathising with, and negotiating agreed decisions with, my peers, decisions that integrate diversity, difference and unity.

• Our ways of knowing are multiple (Heron, 1992, 1996a). First we have experiential knowing: by meeting/encounter/engagement with people, places, processes and things – that is, by felt participation in the being of what is present - a process which involves the whole of our embodied being, and is the ground of the next three. Second there is presentational knowing: by intuitive grasp of the meaning of the patterns and forms of nonverbal imagery, as in the various arts, in immediate perceiving, in memory and dreams. Third we have our very familiar propositional, conceptual knowing, mediated by language. And fourth there's practical knowing: knowing how to do things, manifest in a whole array of skills and competencies - spiritual, psychic, aesthetic, intellectual, political, interpersonal, emotional, technical, clinical, etc. All these modalities, interacting in mutual enhancement, are at the service of mediating divine polarities.

## Axiology

These various polarity properties together generate a theory of value about the divine process. The intrinsic values it enshrines are those of meaning, relationship and creativity: transcendent meaning, situational relationship, and emergent creativity. In traditional language: wisdom, love and power, the equivalency and equipoise of divine attributes.

# 8 Divine inquiry and spiritual inquiry

Divine inquiry is a much wider notion about human relation with the divine than spiritual inquiry. Since the divine is a body-mind - an integration of the manifest, phenomenal and subtle, and the conscious animation I call the spiritual - divine inquiry for humans includes both *manifest inquiry*, and *spiritual inquiry*.

## Manifest inquiry

Manifest inquiry includes all the ways of inquiring, both theoretically and technologically, into the nature and potentials of the manifest realms, both phenomenal and subtle, and of the various entities and processes within them.

- Phenomenal inquiry includes both the social and physical sciences.

- Subtle inquiry includes various forms of psychical and paraphysical research.

The whole scientific enterprise of the modern age is an expression of divine inquiry in its physical phenomenal manifest mode. This is exactly how the founding fathers of modern science such as Kepler and Newton saw it; and how the more recent founding father of modern quantitative psychology, Fechner, saw it.

Inquiry into the relation between the physical sciences and the subtle sciences is still largely underdeveloped. The notion of a subtle ethereal medium certainly played a prominent part in the *speculations* of the founders of modern science (Burtt, 1925). Descartes, Boyle, Gilbert, Newton in the 17th century all take seriously the probable role of the ether as a basis of a variety of physical phenomena. But the ether concept finally disappeared from the conventional scientific view in Einstein's special theory of relativity in 1905.

It is perhaps an error to suppose that self-sufficient enlightenment can be attained about the manifest realms entirely by physical science, to the virtual exclusion of subtle science and any kind of spiritual inquiry.

## Spiritual inquiry

Spiritual inquiry is about opening to and acting with spirit in its three modes of the situational, the immanent and the transcendent.

For the past three thousand years it has been largely focused on the transcendent mode. This monopolar quest has been profoundly fruitful and has bequeathed us a luminous legacy And yet it is today surely an error to suppose that any kind of ultimate spiritual enlightenment can be attained exclusively by inquiry into transcendent spirit, with virtually no manifest inquiry, and no inquiry into spirit as situational and immanent.

Current professions of such end-state enlightenment, based exclusively on limited kinds of dissociated spiritual practice, seem to be for purposes of setting up authoritarian spiritual fiefdoms, whose subjects are led to subscribe to unbalanced monopolar notions of the divine.

## Integrated inquiry

Collaborative action research, in the form of co-operative inquiry, integrates a social science form of manifest inquiry with comprehensive tri-modal spiritual inquiry. I shall continue to call this integrated form 'spiritual inquiry' with the understanding that it is inquiry into the spirit that is:

- The living dynamic ground of our embodiment.

- The reality of our here and now relating to persons and our world.

- The transcendent consciousness embracing our everyday awareness.

## Performative, collaborative action research

Spiritual inquiry, then, relates to spirit in its three modes of the situational, the immanent and the transcendent, as socially embodied and manifest here and now in this situation where we are.

This inquiry is performative, a form of action research, by each of us individually and groups of us co-operatively. By participating in spirit in the fullness of our embodied situation, we co-create with it our realization of it. As we meet spirit, we shape it as it shapes our shaping of it. The spiritual authority for the validity of such co-shaping rests within each of us as critical subjectivity, and between us as critical intersubjectivity. The autonomous judgments of validity which we make in this way - the continuous acts of subtle discrimination - are co-created with our inner spiritual life and light, in the context of our current state of knowledge and of our resonance with, and our discussions with, each other. They are divine-human judgments, both luminously informative, and also contingent, maculate and relative to their context.

They are both revelatory and fallible. See *Sacred Science* (Heron, 1998: 50-60) and Perspective 17 below.

## The polarity within engagement, enlivenment and enlightenment

Within the vision here put forward, such inquiry has a basic polarity. On the one hand, it is an inquiry about *opening to spirit* as a context of relationship, creativity for living, and meaning. And on the other hand, it is an inquiry into *acting with spirit* to transform relations with humans and other entities, and with our environments, in the phenomenal and subtle realms. This is the polarity, within the process of inquiry, between receptive opening up, and co-creative action. The inquiry is a consummation of human-divine flourishing, a celebration of intimate communion, and of transformative going forth.

Let's consider this receptive-active polarity within each of the three aspects of the spiritual - the situational, the immanent and the transcendent. But first a reminder about how they are defined, and the choice of a name for the inquiry associated with each:

- *The situational.* The presence that is *between* everyone and everything in our current situation, phenomenal and subtle. The living reality of our participative relation with what and with whom is here and now in this place. Spiritual inquiry in relation to the situational I call *engagement.*

- *The immanent.* The spiritual life-potential embedded *within* creation, the indwelling source of manifest becoming, the drive of emergent development. Spiritual inquiry in relation to the immanent I call *enlivenment.*

- *The transcendent.* Cosmic consciousness *beyond* and encompassing creation, and emanating its formative archetypes. Spiritual inquiry in relation to the transcendent I call *enlightenment.* I do not mean by the term 'enlightenment' any kind of final end-state of spiritual realization as in the old traditions, but an ongoing process calling for integration with both engagement and enlivenment, all embodied in our social processes.

If we now take into account the receptive-active polarity, we have three components – each dipolar - of spiritual inquiry, making six in all:

*Engagement*

- Open to the presence-between in this situation.

engaged vital enlightenment

- Act with the presence-between in this situation.

*Enlivenment*

- Open to spiritual life-potential.

- Act with spiritual life-potential.

*Enlightenment*

- Open to transcendent consciousness.

- Act with transcendent consciousness.

Both the *opening* and the *acting* inquire into human-divine co-creation. In opening to spirit we both immediately meet it, and also co-creatively shape it in terms of some kind of symbolic mediation. In acting, the distinct spirit of each of us, as one of the Many, is co-creatively performative with and within the spirit of the One.

These three forms of paired inquiry are mutually supportive and interactive. Engagement is the mediating middle ground between enlivenment and enlightenment and provides the forum for their complementary kinds of opening and co-creation. Thus engagement is the fullness of a collaborative embodied relation with being.

I am here presenting another form of integral transformative inquiry (Leonard and Murphy, 1995). Its goal is collegiality, *sobornost,* individual diversity in free social unity: a consummation of the embodied realization of the Between, grounded in the depths of the immanent, and graced by the embrace of the transcendent.

**Parity, balance and centrality**

I do not believe there is any kind of prescribed, sequential path for the cultivation of the various states of engagement, enlivenment and enlightenment. Relationship, life and light have parity of value, as far as I can see. Each person will evolve their own idiosyncratic way of unfolding each and of them and integrating all of them. All I can commend is that over time, and this may mean over long periods of time, each of them is given parity of attention, and all of them are brought into integral balance. At the same time it is clear that engagement - the realm of human mediation and collaboration – is central, since this where we always already are.

In the three Perspectives that follow, I outline twelve basic components of spiritual inquiry, which do not claim to be exhaustive. There are two for each of the six bulleted points above. As forms of inquiry each reader needs to modify them to make them suit his or her own approach in a meaningful way. They are certainly not prescriptions for other inquirers, just a contribution to the cartography of spiritual inquiry. They are summarized in Figure 4 in Perspective 11. The twelve are not mutually exclusive, but interweave and overlap, and can be combined in various ways.

# 9 Engagement with situational spirit

The point here is that we enact spirit as the reality of the *between*, that is, of the relation between persons, between persons and other entities of all kinds, and between persons and their physical and subtle environment - in the situation where we are now. On any view of divine-human becoming which actively seeks a balanced integration of the Many and the One, the central enactive locus of spirit is situational and collegial. It is in the here and now experiential occasion where some of the Many - humans and other entities - and the One co-enact free diversity in unity. So central spiritual inquiry is relational: *opening to*, and *acting with*, the divine spirit that connects persons and other entities in the immediate locality of the here and now.

**Open to the presence-between in this situation**

Here are some receptive inquiries for opening to the reality that connects. The first of these includes the second. 'Only connect' said the novelist E.M.Forster.

*Feeling presence here and now*

This is the root practice of participatory awareness. It is very simple. It means opening to our innate capacity for feeling the presence of places, people and other entities and processes. Through this capacity we directly sense our interconnectedness with whom and with what is in our world, and in other interrelated realms. We feel communion, resonance, attunement, the reality of the go-between spirit in the mutuality of relationship. To share presence is to engage with Shekinah, the local divinity of our process in this time and place.

- *Shekinah* in Hebrew means 'residence', 'dwelling'. In Jewish tradition it is the name for the divine presence as it makes itself known in the material world, 'overshadowing', 'hovering', 'indwelling'. It is also associated with the feminine aspect of the divine, concerned with interpersonal relationships.

- In the mystical system of the Kabbalah, *Shekinah* is linked with the tenth Sefirah of Malkhut and the manifestation of the divine kingdom on earth.

- Here *Shekinah* refers to the spiritual reality that is *between* persons, and *between* persons and their worlds. It is the reality of the relation *between*.

## Seamless perceiving

Feeling presence includes the simplicity of participatory awareness, opening to the *processes* of perceiving and sensing, aware that there is no gap between seer, seeing and seen; between hearer, hearing and heard; between toucher, touching and touched; between us, the world we image in any sensory, and extrasensory, mode and the imaging process; between us, our subjective states and sensations, our body, our percepts, and our world. To perceive a world is to feel, to participate in, an ongoing interfusion of subject and object through sensory and extrasensory imagery, an interfusion which is capable of development and extension and which reveals the *distinctness* of subject and object within their *interactive communion*.

The business of feeling presence and seamless perceiving is not something to be constructed and manufactured. It is a matter of uncovering and noticing what is already going on as an innate condition of our being-in-a-world. We open fully and equally to inner and outer experiences, while letting go of any tight conceptual grip upon them, and at the same time abandoning any compulsive emotional grasp of them. Then we enjoy their seamless marriage within the embrace of being.

## Individual presencing

Feeling presence and seamless perceiving constitute the process of participatory engagement with what and with whom is here and now. This simple and fundamental inquiry can be practised individually any place, any time, in relation with nature and its diverse entities, with human artefacts, with other people, and with subtle realms and subtle entities.

## Collaborative presencing

It becomes a shared transformative inquiry when it is practised collaboratively by all those in a group. Here are a few examples:

- As the awarely shared ground of a conversation, or any other social enterprise at work, at college, at home or at play. This inquiry involves everyone in the skill of double-plane functioning: engaging in the social activity while at the same time dropping down into the "ocean of shared feeling...where we become one with one another" (Alexander, 1979: 294).

- As mutual presencing in a group, inquiring into the ocean of shared feeling as such. We sit close and comfortable, relax physically and mentally, and simply feel our presence with each other and any other beings involved in our communion. Then we become aware of the presence-between-us, a band of golden silence, the Shekinah of our gathering. Our hands may be linked, or not; our eyes may be closed, or open scanning each other's eyes.

- As silent sustained mutual gazing between two of us. In this radical one-to-one inquiry, we can become immersed in our dual-unity, the living spacious reality of the sacred Between savouring the distinctness of each within the unity of our dyad. This mode of access to embodied divinity is rich in ambrosia. It is the universal form of *satsang:* peer to peer transmission of divine presence. The skill required is to let go of emotional tension and to be fully present to each other as whole beings, while deepening this mutual presence into living beatitude - the enjoyment of divine favour.

**Act with the presence-between in this situation**

This active spiritual inquiry is for partners, or any face-to-face group, who meet with the shared intention of transforming their interactions with each other and their world, in any of its manifold aspects, to enhance diversity in free unity, interconnected flourishing.

*Participatory decision-making*

Participatory decision-making integrates autonomy, co-operation and hierarchy. In this inquiry, each person moves between and integrates these three positions, and moves between three phases. There is an autonomous phase: each person states clearly their individual, idiosyncratic preference, in relation to the matter being discussed. Next a hierarchical phase: people start to think integrally on behalf of the whole group, and one or more participants state integral proposals that seek to honour diversity-in-unity, and that resonate strongly with the group. Then there is a co-operative phase of negotiating an agreed decision, after debating, selecting and refining the most resonant integral proposal.

Fundamentally, a co-operative attitude of mutual regard and respect underlies all three phases. They are each exercised, and the movement between them is taken, in attunement with the reality of the go-between spirit of the occasion. Situational spirit is a presence which empowers collegiality - the creative interaction of autonomy, hierarchy and co-operation in human decision-making and action. This is a profound practice: exhilarating, liberating, and challenging participants with the intermittent discomforts of ego-burning.

- For a related approach to peer group decision-making that has a spiritual focus see *PeerSpirit Circling* (Baldwin and Linnea, 2000).

*Life-style transformation*

Participatory decision-making, above, is about the *process* of decision-making. Life-style transformation, in this inquiry practice, brings about the *products* of decision-making, fulfilling in co-operative action inquiry its intended outcomes. It involves transformative deeds covering a wide range of social and environmental outcomes; or some kind of aesthetic, functional or technological product serving such outcomes; or some kind of information gathering or training furthering such outcomes. The collaborative action inquirers are co-creators with divine becoming of planetary transformation, manifest in terms of social justice and human rights, personal and interpersonal development, aesthetic creation and celebration, economic sustainability, ecological balance and cosmic attunement - at home, at work, in the community, and regionally, nationally, internationally and in relation to the wider cosmos. We start here, in this place where we are, with these immediate partners, friends, family, colleagues and associates - and other sentient beings around us.

- For a related account of human-divine co-creativity see the world-view of creation spirituality at *www.creationspirituality.com.*

- "God as Creator is incarnate as self-creating universe, including self-creating creatures within that universe, such as, for instance, ourselves as human beings. Creativity itself is what is evolving in the cosmos, and we are at the growing edge...We are in a position to realize ourselves as incarnate divine creativity." (Beatrice Bruteau, 1997).

- "In co-creation we bring forth two strands - our spiritual essence and our scientific and social capacities - to participate in the creation. When these strands blend, a new human is born; a universal human, a co-creator, a unique and personal expression of the divine." (Hubbard, 1998).

*Life-style transformation* is closely related to *Life-style choices* (see the next Perspective). For full details of these and other sorts of practice applied within a two-person relationship see Langton and Heron (2003).

# 10 Enlivenment with immanent spirit

Enlivenment inquiries are about opening to, and co-creatively acting with, the depths within, the spiritual as indwelling potential, the divine ground of our human motivation – our will to live both as a distinct individual and as a universal participant. We open to our intrinsic dynamic rooting in spiritual life-impulse, the wellspring of our energies and capacities, in relation with which we co-create our becoming. Enlivenment is responsiveness to the ground of our incarnate being, the embedded entelechy of all our possibilities.

A fundamental aspect of enlivenment is about opening to and expressing the spiritual potential within the primary energies of our bodily life, that is, within the basic life impulses to breathe, move, sleep, rest, eat, drink, perceive, speak, relate, be sexual. These are all gateways to a spiritually grounded, fully embodied, distinctive and inclusive way of living-in-connectedness. That the vital energies of the body can evoke the living spirit in which they are grounded, and whence they issue forth, is demonstrated in distinctive ways in each of the following:

- The holotropic breathwork of Stan Grof (1988) and the wide range of subtle and spiritual states it delivers.

- The paratheatrical research of Antero Alli (2003) with its comprehensive phenomenology of physical behaviours for cultivating 'resonance with vertical sources'.

- Charismatic education and training (Heron, 1999) in the context of a dipolar account of spirit (Heron, 1998).

- Aspects of the integral transformative practice of Leonard and Murphy (1995).

- The interactive somatic inquiries proposed by Marina Romero and Ramon Albareda (Ferrer, 2003) in their work on a fully embodied and vitalized spiritual life.

- The work of Michael Washburn (2003) asserting spiritual as well as instinctual energy in the Dynamic Ground of the human being, which can be awakened as an enlivening and guiding force within our bodies.

- Jorge Ferrer's (2006) considered affirmation of embodied spirituality.

## Open to spiritual life-potential

*Wellspring evocation*

Find a quiet time and place, sit relaxed with spine erect, feel and image the inner ground in which your immediate current state of being is rooted; inwardly co-enact with spirit, and have a felt sense of, the wellspring, the underlying source of your everyday mental-emotional-motivational life. Speak out loud, or silently within, such declarations as "I open to you, divine wellspring of my lived experience" or "I open to the divine animation that is the root of my motivation". Use any form of words, any metaphor, that opens you up to feel the spacious, generous mystery of indwelling potential.

*Charismatic opening*

Move on the inclination deep within to open your incarnate being - your whole embodied attitude of soul - through breath, gesture, posture, facial expression to the totality of what there is, to the whole presence of Being, manifest here and now in this situation. Add movements, sounds, and declarations that well up from the *hara,* the life-centre in the belly, to affirm your divine gesture. Allow the primary energies of bodily life to unfurl their divinizing power, the indwelling empowering presence of divine animation. This can be experienced as an all-consuming, all-sustaining, all-creating everywhere active experiential fire. This kind of opening can lead over into sustained expressive action as in *primary theatre* below.

## Act with spiritual life-potential

*Life-style choices*

Open up to the liberated place within your embodied being where you can be co-creative with immanent spirit, your animating life-potential, in making life-style choices. You open to the inner spiritual and subtle womb, in the belly of your being, where the generative potency of immanent spirit, divine life, dwells. This womb is the locus of your potential, the source and seedbed of options and possibilities. What emerges from it, when you intend to be co-creative with it, are periodic impulses, prompts, innovations, proactions, responses and reminders, about your personal action, development and relationships within the great web of interbeing.

This active participation in indwelling spiritual entelechy, a sacred soil at the root of embodiment, may generate specific life-style impulses about:

- A feel for empowering rhythms and patterns of behaviour in time and space.

- A sense of fitting and appropriate action within the immediate situation - the content and timing of specific actions relating to personal and shared life-style, social change, spiritual practice and unfoldment, artistic creation, learning and inquiry, the process of inner regression and emotional healing.

These life-style impulses arising within are maculate, contingent, relative both to the limiting situations within which they occur and to your shaping and selective framing of them. To be co-creative with this indwelling animation is to shape and frame it as much as it enacts you.

- Compare the work of McMahon and Campbell (1991), following on from the work of Gendlin (1981). They develop Gendlin's experiential focusing in terms of a bio-spiritual approach, which emphasizes "an experience of grace in the body". They relate letting go into the body-feeling about an issue, the "felt shift", to a movement of the indwelling life-giving presence and power of God.

- Compare also the Japanese tradition of the *hara* and the belly. See Karlfried Graf Von Durckheim (1962).

*Primary theatre and lean ritual*

These inquiries are for sharing with a partner or an ongoing spiritual inquiry group. They build on *charismatic opening* above. In *primary theatre* a person explores, reveals and celebrates, in nonverbal and verbal ways, their original relation with creation. It is based on the view that each human being can properly assert:

- I have my own original relation with being, with what there is.

- Revelation is now, in my immediate present experience of what there is at this time and place.

- Spiritual authority is within me.

- I can use posture, gesture, movement, sound and breath – and all the primary energies of my embodiment - as an original language for exploring and expressing my participation in what there is.

- I can use verbal metaphors to elaborate that expressive language.

- My spiritual enlivenment is an ongoing process, starting now as I open myself to, and actively express, my intrinsic connectedness with what there is.

- I am included within, and am at the crest of, the living process of divine becoming

- This process is greatly enhanced if I resonate with other persons similarly and simultaneously enlivened.

In a small group each person is open idiosyncratically to respond - in resonance with each other - with movement, speech, and sound (vocal and/or with a variety of musical instruments) to the spontaneous promptings of their immanent, indwelling spiritual energy. Or each person can taken equal time for a solo turn, with the supportive attention of the rest of the group.

A *lean ritual* is free of any explicit theology, and uses the primal meaning of basic words and gestures. Thus the group stand in a circle with arms reaching upward and say 'Above', then kneel to touch the ground and say 'Below', then cross their hands over the heart and say 'Within', finally reach out to take the hands of those on either side and say 'Between'. Innumerable versions of a lean ritual can be designed. Lean ritual generates a subtle sense of shared sacred space.

- For more on primary theatre and lean ritual see *www.human-inquiry.com/practices.htm* and *Helping the Client: A Creative, Practical Guide* (Heron, 2001b:112-115). See also Perspective 19 below.

*Charismatic action inquiry* builds on the principles of primary theatre. It is an inquiry into the cultivation of personal power and presence in interaction with other persons. It is relevant for living generally, and in particular for group facilitators and educators - who need to acquire distress-free authority, and to emanate a quality which liberates inner empowerment in those who seek to learn within its ambience.

It is a social skills counterpart to Aikido training. Unlike Aikido, which is a martial art busy with the charismatic toppling of one's opponent, charismatic competence is about being empowered from within the depth's of one's embodiment to be actively present for and with other people in a life-enhancing way.

Charismatic action inquiry works with all the psychophysical modes involved in social interaction: posture, gesture, facial expression, movement, relative position, voice, speech, eye-contact, touch. Charisma is to do with conscious command of all these modes, in dynamic engagement with another person, or with a group of people.

It is grounded in a felt sense, experientially from within, of one's total psychophysical presence in space, simultaneously in every direction and in every mode; an integral felt sense that wells up from the *hara*, the life-centre in the belly. This felt sense infuses spatial orientation and relative position, posture, gesture and movement, the tone and timing of voice, the diction, meaning and social intent of speech. It also infuses surrounding social space and is the ground of empathic resonance with other persons who are present.

• For a full, detailed account of charismatic action inquiry exercises, see Chapter 9, *Living in Two Worlds* (Heron, 2006: 109-125), and Chapter 12, *The Complete Facilitator's Handbook* (Heron, 1999: 215-248).

# 11  Enlightenment with transcendent spirit

Inquiry here is about co-enacting with spirit opening to, and manifesting in action, the spiritual as transcendent, as overarching divine consciousness, informing the manifest and beyond it. We co-enact the emanation of our local consciousness from this encompassing and universal awareness.

## Open to transcendent consciousness

The two inquiries below co-enact with spirit versions of the great reversal, turning about in the deepest seat of the ordinary mind to open to its continuity with universal awareness.

### The lens of attention

Human attention is at the core of everyday awareness: we attend to this and we attend to that. It is the very focus of our effective in-the-world consciousness. Yet when we attend to this attentive capacity, when we rest our focus on itself, it becomes a lens which refracts a vast expanse of transpersonal awareness, a soaring outreach of universal intelligence of which our own attention to daily life is the local manifest. Such vigilant awareness of its own intrinsic stillness opens to the cosmic ocean of consciousness.

We can participate in this consciousness in its several aspects: as the sustaining, managerial intelligence of the universe; as the Logos, creative divine speech which utters the universe; as indeterminate ineffability, beyond all name and form. Or we open to it as the consort embracing Shekinah, the presence of our process in this place, and then we are aware of its intimate union with the here and now realm of situational spirit.

### Transcendental subjectivity

Another version of the great reversal is via our experience of 'I', that subjective unity of our consciousness on which all coherence and meaning of inner and outer experience depend. The 'I' transcends any account it gives of itself, since it is the ever-present pre-condition of every account. When we attend to the 'I', open to the 'I', beyond any determinate description of itself, we open to its emanation from, its consubstantiality with, the transcendent I AM, that divine consciousness that embraces whatever there is. This is one-One consubstantiality: since the 'I' can always give an appropriate developing account of itself, it is a distinct one of the Many; since it always absolutely transcends this account, it is contained in the One. This consubstantiality dwells in the spiritual heart. This too closes the circle and takes us back to the spiritual heart in the first of the twelve inquiries, feeling presence here and now.

## Act with transcendent consciousness

The next two inquiries relate to the spiritual as transcendent Logos, the divine speech which declares the universe.

### *Refraction of archetypal powers and presences*

One form of dynamic, active inquiry into such consciousness is to refract the original utterance of creation which it emanates, to echo the cosmos-creating archetypes of the divine word. We invoke, commune with, and actively radiate with, elevated presences (hyper persons) in subtle dimensions, presences who mediate, in a numinous, luminous and sounding way, divine powers - the archetypal formative principles of creation. Within this communion, and through our ritual acts and declarations, we refract the powers within our own phenomenal context, giving them additional local boost or impact.

We are here participating actively in the realm of Plato's forms; the powers of Philo; the interpenetrating living intelligences of Plotinus's *nous*; the *mundus imaginalis*, the *alam al-withal* of the Sufis; divine imaginals in the writings of Douglas Fawcett; angel communion in the Christian tradition.

- For a more detailed account of some provisional working hypotheses involved in this sort of inquiry, see the section on *Subtle activism* at the end of this Perspective.

- For a full account of an ongoing inquiry which combines elements of inquiry drawn from the modalities of engagement, enlivenment and enlightenment see Perspective 19 and Heron and Lahood (2008).

### *Illuminated language*

In this inquiry, through the spoken and the written word we manifest ostensive definition that transcends itself. We use language as a vehicle for pointing to that which both originates it and goes beyond it. We speak and write of that which is boundless beyond space, light beyond differentiated light, uncaused, uncreated, unborn, unconditioned, ineffable, beyond all name and form, free of all determination – and…a creative source of all determinate form and process. We celebrate through the performative word the self-transcending creativity of the original Word.

Here is a table summarizing the framework of the twelve inquiry practices described in this and the previous two Perspectives.

|  | **Immanent life** | **Situational presence** | **Transcendent consciousness** |
|---|---|---|---|
| Opening | Wellspring evocation<br><br>Charismatic opening | Feeling presence<br><br>Seamless perceiving | Lens of attention<br><br>Transcendental subjectivity |
| Acting | Life-style choices<br><br>Primary theatre & lean ritual | Participatory decision- making<br><br>Life-style transformation | Refracting powers & presences<br><br>Illuminated language |
|  | *Enlivenment* | *Engagement* | *Enlightenment* |

*Figure 4: the three ways*

## A postscript on subtle activism and interior communion

This is my current perspective on what, among other things, may be going on in our long-term inquiry group, when there is an interaction between engagement, enlivenment and enlightenment. It relates to my experiences and the reports of others within our meetings. I set it out in nine uninhibited and very provisional working hypotheses. It is just one belief-system, among several that may co-exist in our group.

1. We are in one vast unified field of spirit in manifestation: spirit embracing consciousness and life, manifestation embracing subtle realms and physical worlds.

2. Each of us is a local eddy of manifest spirit within this greater field, explicitly participating in a given physical locality within it, and tacitly participating in the whole multidimensional field.

3. Each of us is explicitly embodied in a physical body and tacitly embodied in a subtle body. The physical body realizes mortal life and consciousness. The subtle body has the latent capacity for non-mortal life and consciousness.

4. When we awaken to our subtle embodiment and make it explicit within our physical embodiment, our non-mortal life and consciousness infuses and transforms our mortal life and consciousness.

5. We effect this awakening by posture, gesture, movement, rhythm and sound, which both *express* the idiosyncratic promptings of our immanent spiritual life, the animating ground of our double embodiment; and *open up* to immediate theophany - the divine embrace of spirit manifesting here and now in this place.

6. When we effect this awakening together in the same place, combining autonomous individual expression with mutual resonance, we become a potent ring of awakened doubly incarnate beings, and thus open to a space between our physical world and the subtle realms. The space between the worlds is a sacred matrix, the here and now reality of the divine embrace of both realms. We have called it variously Shekinah, and the band of golden silence.

7. When this sacred matrix is opened up by our dynamic toning and gestures, it calls forth participation from presences in subtle realms who interact with us and together with us engage in extraordinary forms of subtle activism. The presences, attuned to archetypal energies, can pour these into our shared and co-energized space, with three principal effects *co-created* with us:

- A transformation of the psychosomatic field of each of us.

- A transformative impact upon the psychosomatic field of the human race, through instant morphic resonance between us and the rest of embodied humanity through specific patterns of genetic, psychological, cultural, historic and subtle affinity.

- An empowering of each of us in the furtherance of our social activism out there in this world.

8. After the dynamic phase of subtle activism, we have a potent phase of stillness, standing or being seated within the band of golden silence, the Shekinah matrix. In this ecstatic communion, we seem to open to the reality between us, to the divinity that is an ever-present flame of unity here and now where we are. This silent communion is complementary to the subtle activism and makes a very fundamental contribution indeed to the three kinds of effect described above.

9. It is possible that this complementary combination of subtle activism and interior communion, through its threefold effects, sows the seeds for the future unfolding of doubly incarnate cultures, the birth of civilizations which are both autonomously creative in the human realm, cultivate explicit co-creation between independent humans and peer presences in the subtle realms, and are open to the ever-present reality of the between.

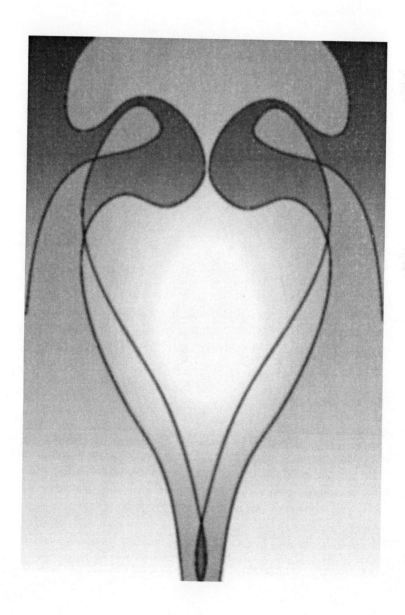

# 12 Presuppositions of spiritual inquiry

## Spiritual education

Spiritual inquiry presupposes that the inquirer:

- Has learned a mother tongue, and has been socialized and educated within a culture.
- Has been spiritually educated, that is, has acquired a working knowledge of conceptual distinctions to do with human spirituality, through some acquaintance with texts, teachers, traditions and schools, ancient and modern.
- Has been spiritually trained, that is, has become proficient in some kind of spiritual practice.
- Knows how to engage in spiritual practice, both alone and with others, as a mode of inquiry.

Spiritual education and training may be acquired in some spiritual school, ancient or modern, or may be self-taught from the literature of some school. Spiritual training within a school is at best a precursor to, and is not the same as, spiritual inquiry. Spiritual inquiry is an advanced form of spiritual practice which requires its own preparation and is outside the aegis of any tradition. See *Sacred Science* (Heron, 1998: 46-49).

In the final analysis, it seems to me that knowing how to make spiritual distinctions, knowing how to engage in spiritual practice, and knowing how to do spiritual inquiry are all part of the same process.

## Authority within

Spiritual inquiry presupposes that each inquirer has an internal monitor, a divine ground within, which is an autonomous touchstone for making valid spiritual distinctions. The beginner may project this inner authority outward for a period and invest it in some external spiritual authority to acquire a training in some type of spiritual practice. But spiritual inquiry as such presupposes that such projection is withdrawn, and that all texts, teachers, schools and traditions of belief and practice, become valuable secondary resources for the inquiry process. The primary resource is a creative interpretation, within the limits of one's current state and context, of the promptings of divine becoming - the *deus implicitus,* the divine roots of human aspiration, spirit-in-action - deep within. Spiritual inquiry, with this primary resource, is a radical and fundamental form of spiritual practice. It involves the co-creation of a spiritual path by the discriminating inquirer-in-context and the *deus implicitus.* For a fuller account of the authority within see Perspective 17 below, and *Sacred Science* (Heron, 1998: Chapter 3).

## Human-divine enaction

The spiritual inquiry process presupposes enaction, that is, the integration of ideational construction and direct encounter with the divine. Without ideational distinctions about divine reality and human spirituality, we cannot guide and conduct the inquiry process. Without unmediated touch with divine reality, in some respect or other, our constructions are unwarranted. Spiritual inquiry makes subtle distinctions in order to meet the divine that is. So our enactions involve mediated-immediacy, the interfused relation of human cognitions and divine presence. We both interpret divine reality and at the same time commune with it. The fruits of spiritual inquiry are human-divine co-creations.

## Fallibility and revelation

Spiritual inquiry is both fallible and revelatory in varying degrees. It is highly fallible when human mediation distorts divine immediacy. It is highly revelatory when human mediation clarifies its communion with divine immediacy, and when divine immediacy enhances human mediation.

## Relative-universal truth

Spiritual inquiry presupposes a relative-universal view of truth. In so far as our spiritual cognitions are mediated, their claims to truth are relative to the historical, cultural and immediate social and personal context within which that mediation is generated. In so far as we have adopted procedures to clarify our mediations and ground them in co-creation with divine immediacy, our cognitions can lay a modest claim to have a bearing on what is universal. But what is universal is Many-One, diversity in free unity, so what is universal is not only a unity but also a diversity of enacted attributes.

## Divine becoming

Spiritual inquiry presupposes a divine reality which is greater than, and subsumes, the inquiry process, and which is the totality of what there is in every respect, including divine becoming. And the inquiry process, as human-divine co-creation, is itself a part of, a participant in, this divine becoming.

## Innovation and diversity

Spiritual inquiry presupposes that it is intrinsically innovative. It necessarily transcends any account it gives itself of its predetermined limits as to what and how and when it can know divine reality. It can progressively recreate its own enactions about its divine scope. It is free, self-caused, divinely intelligent activity, and is at the leading edge of divine becoming among the Many. Since its account of the divine is a free co-creation of the inquirer in communion with the divine - a communion between one of the Many becoming and the One - the diversity in these accounts is likely to be as significant as the unity and universality.

## Determinate and indeterminate

Spiritual inquiry presupposes within divine reality the interplay of the determinate and the indeterminate, the conservative and the innovative. Without determinate, constant features of divine reality, there is no intelligible context for the emergence of the spiritually innovative, which will, of course, progressively transform its conservative context. But any account an inquiry gives of these (and any other) polar parameters - that they are, and what they are - is itself an enaction, open to evaluation in terms of its fallible/revelatory status.

## Dialogue

Hence spiritual inquiry presupposes a requirement of dialogue. It can only manifest in the limited and finite enactions of individuals and groups, and needs the mutual correction and enrichment of diverse overlapping perspectives. Particularly important here is gender dialogue.

## Extended epistemology and the primacy of the practical

Spiritual inquiry also presupposes a requirement of an extended epistemology - holistic cognition. It needs the totality of ways of knowing to acquaint it with the fullness of divine reality. So it involves knowing-how, knowing-that, knowing-as and knowing-with - practical, conceptual, imaginal and affective ways of knowing (Heron, 1992, 1996a). Practical knowledge, knowing how to act in human-divine co-creation, is the creative consummation of these ways of knowing.

# 13 The authoritarian blight

In this Perspective I examine the role of authoritarianism and its consequences in religious traditions and spiritual schools, ancient and modern.

## Personal witness

All traditions and schools ultimately refer back, whether by first-hand, second-hand or multiple-hand reports, to the personal witness of mystics, ecstatics, religious practitioners themselves, revealed through their words, their deeds and their presence.

## Spiritual innovation and tradition

Mystics engage in an inner journey, which includes a necessary element of experiential inquiry, since subtle discrimination needs to be exercised at critical points. But the journey is also set within a given spiritual tradition and guided by a living teacher. So the inquiry component is severely limited and constrained. The exercise of inner discrimination is subordinate to the categories, claims, definitions and demands of the tradition. Indeed, in oriental traditions the capacity for such discrimination is subjected to long periods of scriptural indoctrination and conditioning, before any meditative practice commences. The neophyte is taught what experiential distinctions to make prior to having any relevant experience.

> In most traditions - such as Advaita Vedanta and many Buddhist schools - a period, usually lasting several years, of rigorous study of the spiritual scriptures and 'right views' is regarded as a prerequisite for meditative practice and experiential enactment of the teachings. The immersion in experiential practices without an appropriate understanding of the teachings is regarded not only as premature, but also pointless and potentially problematic. (Ferrer, 1998)

The result of this sort of thing is that budding practitioners, within established religious traditions both east and west, have the kinds of experiences that they have been taught to have.

Some mystics, however, are primitive and solitary pioneers of a more authentic spiritual inquiry. They apply to the mystical quest a limited version of autonomous lived inquiry together with careful phenomenological reporting. They rise out of the immediate constraints of local religious tradition, eastern or western, and originally define or redefine the territory of spiritual experience. Such revision, however, is still limited. It is necessarily restricted to an innovative rearrangement of traditional elements, with some fruitful additions. It inescapably bears the limiting hall marks of the prevailing culture and Zeitgeist.

## The authoritarian blight

Furthermore, the mystic innovators usually become authoritarian when they start a teaching career to pass on their realizations; and their followers will in any case rapidly turn them into authority figures. This is because the only model of spiritual education and training the world has ever known is authoritarian. Thus a sectarian culture is formed, and what is taught within it is given a warrant of authority via an appeal to a combination of some of the following:

- The teacher's intuitive and experiential certitude or faith.

- Divine revelation.

- Instruction from the gods/angels/ancestors/entities.

- Sacred scriptures.

- Established doctrine and practice.

- A lineage of gurus, teachers or priests within the sect.

- An ancient or modern innovative sage or religious founder.

Religious training everywhere, from the remote past to the immediate present, means believing-and-doing what an authority prescribes. A warrant of authority means that when an inquirer asks why they should believe-and-do what is taught, the teacher's reply is, "Because the tradition of which I am a representative says so. And if you follow its teaching, as I and my predecessors have, you will find that it is correct".

This appeal to the weight of established thought and practice proves that it is durable. It does not show that it is valid. Equally, of course, it does not show that it is invalid. It just doesn't answer the inquirer's question. It is beside the point, for the question is an early sign of the inquirer's spiritual autonomy stirring from its life-long slumber. The question cannot be answered from without, but only from the full awakening and alertness of divine autonomy within.

The universal authoritarian tendency within the diverse religious schools, ancient and modern, of our planet, is presumably to do with the remarkable call of the religious quest, which initially throws up a great deal of insecurity. No better way to put a stop to the upsurge of such shakiness - and the underlying challenge of finding an inner source of guidance - than by capping it with allegiance to an external source of certitude. This is the process of spiritual projection, which I discuss in the next Perspective. The institutionalization of this process has had a range of unfortunate consequences *within* each school that maintains it. Let me overstate the case, but only somewhat, in outlining these consequences.

*Hypocrisy*

Little attention is paid to the disturbed behaviour of current authority figures within the sect, to the impact of unprocessed emotional distress on their motivation, their practices, their teachings and their relations with their followers. To take but one example, sexual hypocrisy and perversion is regular scandal among religious authority figures, from Roman Catholic cardinals, bishops and priests, through Muslim mullahs and imams, to oriental gurus such as Swami Muktananda and Sai Baba.

*Spiritual pathology*

It is only very recently that a working distinction has been made between a truly transformative spirituality and a false, psychologically unhealthy, spirituality, of which two kinds can be distinguished. There is repressive spirituality, in which spiritual beliefs and practices are used to reinforce the denial of whole parts of oneself. There is oppressive spirituality, in which inflated spiritual claims are made in order to manipulate, constrain and dominate others to support and follow the claimant (Battista, 1996). And the oppressive kind is itself rooted in the underlying repressive kind. It is a major issue as to the extent to which all past spirituality is riddled with these pathologies, which breed compulsive authoritarianism.

*The dissociation test*

In connection with repressive spirituality, one test proposed by Jorge Ferrer (2002) for determining valid systems of spiritual belief and practice is the dissociation test. This asks whether the system promotes embodied or disembodied spirituality, and favours the embodied approach to being spiritual. Here is Ferrer making his point:

In the wake of our spiritual history, I suggest that 'disembodied' does not denote that the body and its vital/primary energies were ignored in religious practice—they definitely were not—but rather that they were not considered legitimate or reliable sources of spiritual insight in their own right. In other words, body and instinct have not generally been regarded as capable of collaborating as equals with heart, mind, and consciousness in the attainment of spiritual realization and liberation. What is more, many religious traditions and schools believed that the body and the primary world (and aspects of the heart, such as certain passions) were actually a hindrance to spiritual flourishing—a view that often led to the repression, regulation, or transformation of these worlds at the service of the 'higher' goals of a spiritualized consciousness. This is why disembodied spirituality often crystallized in a 'heart-chakra-up' spiritual life that was based preeminently in the mental and/or emotional access to transcendent consciousness and that tended to overlook spiritual sources immanent in the body, nature, and matter.

Embodied spirituality, in contrast, views all human dimensions—body, vital, heart, mind, and consciousness—as equal partners in bringing self, community, and world into a fuller alignment with the Mystery out of which everything arises. Far from being an obstacle, this approach sees the engagement of the body and its vital/primary energies as crucial for not only a thorough spiritual transformation, but also the creative exploration of expanded forms of spiritual freedom. The consecration of the whole person leads naturally to the cultivation of a 'full-chakra' spirituality that seeks to make all human attributes permeable to the presence of both immanent and transcendent spiritual energies. This does not mean that embodied spirituality ignores the need to emancipate body and instinct from possible alienating tendencies; rather, it means that *all* human dimensions—not just somatic and primary ones—are recognized to be not only possibly alienated, but also equally capable of sharing freely in the unfolding life of the Mystery here on earth.

The contrast between 'sublimation' and 'integration' can help to clarify this distinction. In *sublimation*, the energy of one human dimension is used to amplify, expand, or transform the faculties of another dimension. This is the case, for example, when a celibate monk sublimates sexual desire as a catalyst for spiritual breakthrough or to increase the devotional love of the heart, or when a tantric practitioner uses vital/sexual energies as fuel to catapult consciousness into disembodied, transcendent, or even transhuman states of being. In contrast, the *integration* of two human dimensions entails a mutual transformation, or 'sacred marriage', of their essential energies. For example, the integration of consciousness and the vital world makes the former more embodied, vitalized, and even eroticized, and grants the latter an intelligent evolutionary direction beyond its biologically driven instincts. Roughly speaking, we could say that sublimation is a mark of disembodied spirituality, and integration is a goal of embodied spirituality (Ferrer, 2006).

*Dissociation and hierarchical authority*

There is clearly a close connection between dissociated, disembodied spirituality and spiritual authoritarianism. Moreover, the fact that there is so much spiritual authoritarianism in the world, in creeds and cults both old and new, creates a deep attitudinal warp in people which makes them susceptible to oppression by many other kinds of external authority. In reviewing criticisms of the traditional hierarchical model of spiritual reality, promoted by current adherents of the perennial philosophy, Donald Rothberg writes:

> Hierarchical ontologies are commonly ideological expressions of social and psychological relations involving domination and exploitation - of most humans (especially women, workers, and tribal people), of nature, and of certain parts of the self. Such domination limits drastically the autonomy and potential of most of the inhabitants of the human and natural worlds, justifying material inequalities and preventing that free and open discourse which is the end of a free society. It distorts psychological life by repressing, albeit in the name of wisdom and sanctity, aspects of ourselves whose full expression is necessary to full psychological health and well-being. (Rothberg, 1986: 16)

What we need is a diagnostic pathology which allows that a person can be genuinely attuned to one aspect of god, but in a way which entails two errors: first, the experience is sustained in a fixated way that is a defense against attending to some other aspect of the divine; and therefore, second, it is claimed to be much more than it is, and is distorted and inflated to ultimate proportions. Thus the problems with the classic nondual state are its monopolar fixation, its dissociation from active charismatic participation in the social process of divine life and divine becoming, the deluded end-state claims made for it, its gender bias, and its internal association with spiritual authoritarianism.

*The exploitation of spiritual projection*

Relatedly, little attention is paid to the way current authority figures elicit and subtly or brazenly exploit the internal spiritual authority that is unwittingly projected on to them by their followers. Authoritarian abuse of power by leaders and teachers is an invariable consequence of such projection, and there is widespread evidence of ideological, organizational, sexual, financial and bullying abuse in current spiritual movements, whether of ancient or recent origin, whether eastern and western. The spread of Zen and Tibetan institutions in the USA provides a telling example (Lachs, 1994). I discuss the dynamic of spiritual projection in the next Perspective.

*Cultural contamination*

Little attention is paid to the limiting impact, on doctrine and practice, of the worldview of the culture and Zeitgeist prevailing at the time of the origination of a religious tradition by its founder. And, even more so than with current authority figures, the pathological elements in the spirituality of founding sages and 'heroes' go unnoticed.

*Shortfall on criteria*

Little attention is paid to generating criteria to evaluate the overall soundness of a school: its beliefs, practices, teaching methods, initiation procedures, social and political structure, financial basis, claims of its founder, personal behaviour of current authority figures, and so on. It is only very recently that information on the relevant kind of criteria to apply to spiritual schools and cults has had any impact, especially via the internet.

*Disregard of the discarnate context*

No attention is paid to the unseen ambience, the spiritualistic context, of what goes on in a spiritual school or church, that is, to the influence - benign, murky or malign - of discarnate persons on its activities. As long as this kind of influence is ridiculed, denied, occluded and hence unknown, no sect can have any proper claim to understand fully what is going on within its culture. Before going to a week-end retreat with Muktananda, I once saw clairvoyantly a host of associated minions in the next world seeking psychically to prompt humans into attending the event.

*Credulity about channelling*

Where a cult is based on channelling from some discarnate entity, the status of the entity will become the peg for unaware projections, rather than a focus of critical scrutiny.

*Suppression of spiritual autonomy*

Most fundamentally, perhaps, no really serious attention is paid to the ground of discriminating spiritual authority within each student, disciple, or church follower. Any school or tradition that claims any kind of established authority for its teachings and practices will not encourage a full flowering of the autonomous spiritual judgement of each of its followers. Critical subjectivity, individual discriminating practice, independent judgement, inner-directed unfoldment, personal freedom of spirit in defining spiritual reality and in choosing and shaping the spiritual path - all this is discreetly side-stepped or blatantly suppressed or seductively hijacked or, at the very best, affirmed only to be contained within carefully prescribed limits.

The last point leads us again into the topic of the next Perspective, the process of spiritual projection, the displacement of internal authority on to an external source.

# 14 Spiritual projection and authority

## The interior monitor

If you claim that spiritual authority resides in some other person, being, doctrine, book, school or church, you are the legitimating author of this claim. You choose to regard it as valid. No authority resides in anything external unless you first decide to confer that authority on it. Nothing out there is accredited and definitive until you first elect it to be so. All explicit judgements that illumination resides without, rest upon a prior and much more basic tacit light within. When it is made explicit, this is the internal authority of which your own discriminating judgement is the expression. Individual human judgement, with its inner spiritual ground, is the legitimating source of all external spiritual authority. The religious history of the human race appears to involve the slow and painful realization that this is indeed the case.

> We have to realize that every revelation must finally be appropriated by the individual soul. The very term 'revelation' implies the existence of the minds by which it is received. And it is on the attitude of such minds that everything in the end depends. The last word is with the interior monitor. The process is not completed until the divine which appears without is acknowledged by the divine which is enthroned deep within. And no amount of ingenious sophistry can do away with this ultimate fact. In other words the individual must take his stand upon the witness of the inner light, the authority within his own soul. This principle was clearly formulated by the Cambridge Platonist, Benjamin Whichcote, who ventured on the statement: "If you have a revelation from God, I must have a revelation from God too before I can believe you". (Hyde, 1949: 39)

When you are aware that the final court of spiritual authority resides within, and that any authority you have vested in anyone or anything external has derived from the imprimatur of that inner court, then you are spiritually centred and will not in the future become improperly subservient to any religious school or teacher. But when you are not aware of this, then you are busy with spiritual projection, and are spiritually off-centre. The spiritual authority that resides within is not known for what it is, is in some sense suppressed and denied, and is then unawarely projected on, invested in, *and inevitably misrepresented and distorted by,* what is without.

## Projection: perceptual and spiritual

On the view that all realities are subjective-objective, any view that reality is independently objective has a suppressed and unacknowledged subjective component which is prior, and which is inevitably misrepresented by the purely objective account. So in perceiving a world, if the subjective process of visual imaging is displaced and projected out as an objective image, then the subject is misrepresented as a dissociated Cartesian ego peering out at an independent world, instead of being known as a presence in mutual participative engagement with other presences in a shared world. In the same way, if my internal authorizing of a spiritual teacher is displaced and projected out as an external authority residing in that teacher, then my inner authority is misrepresented as nescience seeking illumination from another, instead of being affirmed as my inner knowing seeking dialogue with the inner knowing of another.

Now both sorts of projection, the perceptual and the spiritual, yield benefits up to a point, but sooner or later break down because they try to make a half-truth represent a whole-truth. The critical turning point is when the process of projection becomes conscious and the subject reclaims the personal power within. This doesn't put a stop to the projective process, but it thoroughly reduces it and brings it within the aegis of critical subjectivity. It can now be monitored and modified.

## Projection and the guru

There is no doubt that the process of spiritual projection has been virtually the sole means of spiritual development both for the great mass of mankind and for many of the small minority with serious mystical intent. Indeed, eastern mysticism makes an explicit virtue of it. The guru without represents the guru within, and the guru within is only developed by full allegiance to, and identification with, the guru without. Today, however, in a world of mass communication and planetary information exchange, the competing claims of innumerable spiritual authorities of all kinds stand revealed as a composite Tower of Babel, a noisy confusion of tongues which are missing the inner point.

Spiritual authorities, who are themselves off-centre, have no authentic spiritual autonomy as a basis for real religious co-operation with each other. Their continued spiritual projection - their allegiance to the authority of traditional belief and practice - keeps them apart. There is no co-operation among those who believe, by virtue of traditional indoctrination, that they are one of the god-realized of their respective traditions.

An ecumenical movement among eastern-style perfected masters is not only unheard of, it is in the nature of the case impossible. There are, of course, exceptions among traditions that make more modest claims for their representatives. Christian creeds, all of which keep more of a distance from god, keep having a go at ecumenical togetherness, but their different traditional allegiances permit only the attempt at, not the substance of, religious co-operation.

## Four stages of projection

Here is my working hypothesis about the process of spiritual projection, based on my own involvement with it in different contexts, discussions with friends and colleagues about their inner journey, and on reflections on spiritual psychology. There appear to be four stages in the process, from total projection to its substantial, but not total, withdrawal:

### Intolerance

When the projection is blind and wholly unaware, the devotee is dogmatic and intolerant, outlawing and attacking all other creeds. The spiritual ground within is severely repressed and denied, and the resultant frustration is displaced into the spiritual oppression of alien beliefs.

### Toleration

When there is limited awareness of the projection, we have the anomaly of (1) personal allegiance to the authority projected onto one's own school or church, combined with (2) religious toleration and freedom as between different creeds. In other words, you respect and accept the fact that what is authoritative for you is not so for other people with their diverse beliefs, but fail fully to grasp that this is so because you and they are still busy projecting inner authority outward.

The most extreme version of this anomaly is when you both respect fully the right of other people to vest authority in any creed they choose, and at the same time vest your own authority in a cult that continually denigrates the exercise of your autonomous spiritual judgement.

### Collusion

When there is rather more awareness of spiritual projection, we have an unfortunate anomaly much practised by contemporary authoritarian spiritual teachers, and colluded with by their followers. The teachers repetitively define and prescribe things spiritual, while also repeatedly affirming that authority lies within each follower, who is exhorted to take nothing on teacher say-so but check it out through personal experience. The effect is hypnotic and seductive. The follower comes to believe that what he or she is being taught is also being confirmed from within. But what is within the follower is never encouraged, in it own terms and on its own terms, to define or direct anything spiritual. All definition and direction remain firmly in the hands of the teacher. At the same time as inner discrimination is being encouraged, the person is being told what to believe and to do, and is thus lulled seductively into acquiescent projection.

This anomaly has its degenerate apotheosis in the case of the advanced conventional practitioner, the supposed enlightened one who uncritically directs all his practice and construes all his experience in the terms of tradition with which he has been indoctrinated and which he has internalized, and which has long since usurped the voice of authentic inner discrimination. What he has thus internalized may lead him to believe that he is now one of the god-realized, at an end-stage of enlightenment. Such a person will be benignly and inescapably autocratic in ruling the roost in his or her school of practice, while ostensibly encouraging disciples to make rigorous experiential tests of what is taught.

*Freedom*

When you are fully aware of spiritual projection so that it can be substantially withdrawn and undone, then the spiritual path itself is based on internal authority through the continuous exercise of your own discriminating judgement and its spiritual ground; and this in association with others similarly engaged. Divine becoming emerges as the living spiritual ground of human autonomy and co-operation. And the divinity thus manifest will be significantly different, I believe, in terms of beliefs and practices, from all divinities defined by external authorities. However, there are three very important caveats about all this, the second being the crucial one.

First, such withdrawal is not an all or nothing phenomenon. It may involve a variety of hybrids. These include:

*Sequential projection*

A person projects for a period on one spiritual school, then withdraws it and projects on to another, going through several over a number of years. This process may become quite intentional, in the sense that the person consciously goes along with the authoritarian tendency of a school in order to benefit from its teachings and practices, and pulls out when that tendency becomes too restricting.

*Partial projection*

A person stays constantly within one tradition in allegiance to certain strands of it, while radically reappraising other strands.

*Intellectual freedom*

The intellect appears to exercise a lot of freedom, for example, with respect to transpersonal theory, but practice remains firmly wedded to a traditional school. The theoretical outcome will then include veiled special pleading for the practical allegiance.

*Discreet freedom*

A person remains within one tradition for purposes of the support found within its spiritual community, otherwise picks and chooses among its beliefs and practices, refracting them through the prism of the internal monitor.

Second, and crucially, I do not think there is any such thing as a final end to, a total freedom from, spiritual projection. There is certainly a critical point when it is raised into consciousness and radically withdrawn as personal power is reclaimed. But this reclamation, this radical reappraisal of one's spirituality, necessarily includes elements drawn from past and present spiritual practitioners and thinkers. So the reappraisal weeds out past projections while relying, in part, on new ones in order to do so. The difference, of course, is in the awareness that this going on. Hence the critical subjectivity of a reframing mind, which continually deconstructs presumed internal authority to uncover the projections at work within it. The authority within is never final, always provisional and fallible. I return to this theme in Perspective 17.

Thirdly, the substantial withdrawal of spiritual projection from traditional schools certainly does not mean that one ceases to take account of them and learn anything from them. I have on occasion been criticized on the grounds that my approach to spiritual inquiry is to eliminate from consideration almost everything which has been written on the subject up to now. This is a gross misrepresentation, and quite the opposite of what I believe, which is that the beliefs and practices of the various mystical traditions constitute a huge data-bank, a massive resource which, when treated with due caveats, can be drawn upon, modified and revised in framing the maps which guide the examined life and co-operative spiritual inquiry.

I have learnt a great deal from this legacy. I totally ignore it at my peril, just as I unawarely project on to it at my peril. This is an interesting knife-edge. I need to remember that I do not really know for sure what the ancient mystics meant by what they wrote, and that when I read them (often already via a translation) it is how I make sense of them - my inner knowing in dialogue with the text - that is central. If I project this inner knowing out and claim that such and such is what the mystic meant, and claim further that this meaning is a traditional guide to spiritual wisdom, then I am sorely lost in the process of spiritual projection. I am hiding my own light behind the sage's robe to the rear of which it is displaced. I have lost faith with myself. The whole of the current perennial philosophy business seems to me to be beset by this kind of *mauvais foi*.

## The distortions of spiritual projection

When the spiritual authority that resides within is projected on and invested in some external authority, it inevitably becomes misrepresented and distorted. To disown, deny and be unaware of the inner presence is to damage its formative power and this disfiguration is reflected in the teaching of the outer authority that replaces it. From the other side of the equation, if you want to become a spiritual authority for others, then you need a perverse doctrine that invalidates and undermines their intrinsic inner spirit, and will thus lock in with their disfigured projection of it.

The Christian religion maintained its authority for centuries primarily by the corrupt doctrine of original sin, which proposed that human nature is congenitally tainted and depraved, with a proclivity to sinful conduct. The essence of original sin for Augustine (354-430), the most influential figure in Western Christianity, lay in concupiscence, meaning desire in general and sexual lust in particular. He regarded humanity as "a mass of sin, waited upon by death". He identified the "great sin" that lay behind such misery with sex and sexual intercourse. This catastrophic assault on human eroticism deeply undermined people's faith in their own inner life.

It is not surprising that the last twenty years of Augustine's life were dominated by his controversies against the Pelagians, and as a result of his determined opposition, Pelagianism was condemned by the church as a heresy. Pelagius had rejected the idea of original sin as an inherited defect which impaired the freedom of the will.

He believed in a true freedom of the will as the highest human endowment, and held that persons are responsible for and capable of ensuring their own salvation. This optimistic account of human nature, had it spread widely, would have drastically undermined the authority of the early church.

The authority of spiritual schools and lineages in oriental religions rests on the denigrating view that human personhood, far from being a spiritual presence within divine being, reduces to a selfhood which is lost in illusory separateness. At the ordinary, everyday level, the self is nothing but a mass of congealed fear and clinging, all knotted up. At its very highest level, the soul is still *nothing but* a knot, a contraction, which must die to itself, to become absolute spirit (Wilber, 1997: 47). The spiritual teacher who has undone the knot and transcended separateness is the only one to judge whether the contracted disciple has attained any measure of enlightenment. The disciple surrenders to the guru and identifies with the guru to attain *moksha,* spiritual release and liberation from the illusion of selfhood and the bondage of mortal existence. Indeed, the Zen master subjects his students to physical and mental abuse in order to destroy the illusions in which they are imprisoned (Katz, 1978: 44).

So western spiritual authorities invalidate the erotic roots of personal life and eastern spiritual authorities undermine personal consciousness. Both of them are misrepresenting, denying and oppressing, the spiritual potential of personhood which, honoured in fullness, has its flower in personal autonomy and comprehensive connectedness. Between them, they inflict much damage. For spiritual practices based on negative views of human nature, by repressing positive potential, will cause a distorted return of the repressed. Thus the practice, by denying potential good and thus turning it into actual bad, appears to confirm the negative view on which it is based. This is the ancient corruption of patriarchal priestcraft. The priests put about beliefs and practices, and organize their hierarchy in ways, which generate the sins they claim the power to redeem.

The Christian religion tends toward a modified dualism. It regards the human world as a fallen creation outside god, although he is intimately connected with it. And it regards its priests as appointed by god with authority to mediate in Christ's name on behalf of fallen humanity. Eastern religions tend toward acosmic monism: the world and the human are illusory save when known to be identical with absolute spirit. And the enlightened who know this have absolute authority with regard to the salvation of the unenlightened, who are too identified with the illusion to effect self-liberation. What we see at work, both west and east, is the classic autocracy of spiritual patriarchy. There is no hint of, no interest in, the sacral reality of womankind: embodiment as a primary source of sacrality (Raphael, 1994: 519-20).

## Authoritarian displacement and narcissism

The authoritarian spiritual teacher is also busy, of course, in suppressing some aspects of his or her own authentic inner light and inner life. The resultant subtle frustrations are displaced, acted out, not only in controlling the spiritual path for other people, but also in more or less frequent episodes of verbal, physical, sexual, power-play, and financial abuse of followers.

> The behaviour of teachers, both Oriental and Western, participating in the dramatic spread of Zen and Tibetan institutions in America has often fallen severely short of the ethical ideal. (Crook, 1996: 15)

The stories are legion, and likely to be found in all authoritarian spiritual schools, ancient and modern, eastern and western. They are hushed up for as long as possible, and rationalized by devotees as consciousness-raising tests and challenges. But sooner or later they demand understanding in terms of what they are: evidence of distortions stemming from a neglected spiritual process within the directive teacher. Such distortions exhibit gross and crude forms of spiritual narcissism in the very process whereby the teacher claims he is interrupting it in others.

---

Perspectives 13 and 14 are adapted from the text of Chapter 2 of *Sacred Science* (Heron, 1998).

id
l(
:<

# 15  A religion that has human authority

## Autonomous judgement

Autonomous human judgement is the final and inalienable arbiter of what God is or is not, and whether God is or is not. I cannot get beyond or behind the creative, responsible exercise of my judgement on matters of such fundamental concern. I cannot exempt myself or others from such exercise by appeal to any authority, revelation or source that is eccentric to my judgement, since the adoption of such a source as valid rests on the tacit exercise of my judgement. The inescapably human focus of any religious viewpoint makes all theological pronouncements fallible, and in principle open to revision and restatement.

Such judgement is necessarily rooted in autonomous experience. A valid religion for persons has its primary and continuous source in individual and shared experience, in direct encounter with what is manifest in transformed states of being and wider reaches of awareness. Deep openness to, and conceptually liberated discrimination of, such encounter is prior to, and the ongoing revisionary basis of, all theologies, interpretative frameworks, organizational structures and ritual practices.

Personal autonomy, distinctness of personal being - the exercise of a degree of creative, imaginative, responsible choice in thought, in action, in the management of feeling, in my life as a whole - is a precondition of religious competence. An autonomous person is primarily accountable to her/himself for how choices are made, how experiences are construed. Without some degree of coherent, developed and distinct personhood, I cannot engage in the kind of encounter, discrimination and judgement that makes religion authentic. This leads to a fruitful developmental paradox: how can I really relate to God unless I am properly autonomous, and how can I be properly autonomous unless I really relate to God?

## Distinctness without separateness

Autonomy and distinctness of personal being is not the same as separateness, alienation, and selfishness of being. To become self-transcending, to enter a heritage of consciousness in which the sense of ego-centredness falls away, is also at the same time to experience autonomy and distinctness of personal being at its most subtle and potent. To enter unitive states of awareness is the consummation of personhood. Encounter with God does not dissolve the sense of being a person; rather it transfigures that sense into its archetypal form. This is a very fundamental piece of phenomenology and philosophy in my religious view. The concept of a transfigured person is more potent and liberating than the concept of a destroyed ego.

Thus transformed states of consciousness, the powers and presences encountered therein, the power and presence encountered as the ground of any state of being, can have an elevating, transmuting, refining, enhancing effect on personhood, elevating autonomy to the status of distinctness of being without separateness from other beings and being-as-such. This grace, this charismatic influence, this regenerating, redeeming potency is available to anyone with an open heart and mind anywhere at any time.

## The celebration of worlds

A valid religion is world-affirmative, life-affirmative, person-affirmative. It does not negate the value and reality of the world, of life, of persons and their needs, capacities and concerns. It affirms that the brilliance of this composite, here and now reality becomes ever more manifest as it is transfigured by wider and deeper vision of other realities inter-related with it.

Religion is thus the celebration on the one hand of differences, distinctnesses, uniquenesses, and on the other hand of how these orchestrate into remarkable wholes. It participates in the variegated dance of beings within Being, delighting in how the dance occurs, for the 'how' contains the 'what' and the 'why'.

Persons are distinct and also inseparably interrelated with the fields of process within which they unfold. The reality of both subject and object, of person and field, lies in part in their interdependence, interdefinability and interconnectedness. Identification of a person's distinctness, while it is not reducible to, is nevertheless inseparable from, identification of the various fields of process within which it emerges.

I hypothesize that there are spaces other than physical spaces, fields of process other than physical fields and the social and psychological phenomena that manifest in physical fields. The investigation of this other reality involves the integration of religion, science and personal development in a new paradigm of inquiry. Physical fields of process and para-physical, subtle fields, together with the persons or presences that are manifest respectively in each, appear to function in some respects in relative independence of each other, and in other respects in relative dependence on each other. We need, through appropriate investigation, to get clearer about this, that is, to respect both the relative functional autonomy, and the relative functional interrelatedness. If this hypothesis is correct, we live in two sorts of world, two sorts of universe at once. We need to identify and take charge of this extraordinary double fact, and not live as if oblivious to the other reality.

**Co-operative inquiry and a self-generating culture**

Cooperative inquiry, or peer experiential research, in which everyone in the inquiry group is both co-researcher and co-subject, is the fitting mode of inquiry for altered states of consciousness and the two worlds hypothesis. Only persons-in-relation-in-their-worlds can find out about persons in relation in their worlds. Persons cannot absent themselves from their immersion in reality in order to inquire into the nature of that reality. The inquirer must undergo the experience being inquired into, but in thoroughgoing research dialogue with others similarly engaged, maintaining all the checks and balances that enhance the validity of the inquiry.

A self-generating culture is one in which persons give meaning to their relation with the world, and find meaning in that relation, through enacting a variety of rituals and ceremonies that affirm and explore the recurring archetypal features of the human condition: birth, puberty, sexual initiation, the starting and ending of partnerships and relationships, death, and many, many more. Included in these are rituals that affirm and explore the reality of the two worlds, their interconnections, their times and seasons of mutual influence; and rituals that celebrate the transcendent unity of the whole.

Such rituals are living theatre, creative improvisation, societal art. They are human creations; they celebrate human reality and the wide, multidimensional ambience within which human reality emerges. Creative experimentation with ritual and ceremony of many new and varied kinds - as art, as celebration - is part of the religious enterprise as I see it (Heron, 1998).

Persons with charismatic gifts, who stand specially poised at the interface between the two worlds, between this reality and the other reality, need encouragement and training to fulfil a potent function in creating a multi-dimensional society familiar with several sorts or levels of reality. Yet apart from special gifts in some persons, every person has a more ultimate charismatic identity, in the sense of having simple access to that source when personhood emerges. And in a community within a self-generating culture, the role and ritual function of Transcendental Witness can be rotated among members, to remind everyone of their own fundamental source and heritage.

## The art of enjoyment and the art of suffering

What I have called peer experiential research is concerned primarily with inquiry, although there is considerable art in participating in and managing the process with others. Ritual in a self-generating culture is concerned primarily with art, although such ritual is an art form which is also at the same time a mode of knowing and inquiry. Not only through ritual, but also through daily living, the art of enjoyment and the art of suffering I see as part of the religious life. Such art involves at least the following:

- Awareness and understanding of what is going on, with some attention free, liberated, outside it, not totally lost or absorbed in it.

- Experience of the pleasure or pain, with some symbolic expression of it and its meaning (or lack of meaning) for the one undergoing it.

- This expression shared in a community of value with others.

One primary feature of the art of enjoyment is sexual intimacy. Religion that has human authority is uncompromisingly sex-positive, in my view. The art of sexual enjoyment is seen as one of the sacraments in living. Religion that acknowledges Goddess as well as God, Shakti as well as Shiva, Kundalini as well as Sushumna or the Path of Brahma, Yin as well as Yang, archetypal femininity as well as archetypal masculinity, will see sexual union as a potential treasure house of cosmogenetic ecstasy and awareness. Mysticism and sex can be desperately cast asunder; or sweetly, subtly and potently united. The latter seems to be a properly religious approach.

One primary feature of the art of suffering is the ability to take charge of the basic sorts of human distress emotions - grief, fear and anger. Very important in handling an overload of these emotions, which many people undoubtedly suffer in ways that distort behaviour and make for unhappiness, is the ability to initiate and sustain cathartic release both in oneself and in others. The restorative, regenerative and healing role of catharsis has always traditionally found its origin and home in religion. And where, in an ostensibly secular setting, human beings nowadays learn to elicit and manage the catharsis of their own very human distress, there also a subtle religious mood is created. But traditional religions initiated and legitimated cathartic episodes to a very limited degree, while displacing denied distress into restrictive authoritarianism.

Today, when catharsis of more humanistic scope is initiated and legitimated by autonomous humans, a climate is generated for the emergence of a non-dogmatic, non-authoritarian religion in which art, celebration, inquiry, and the management of political and practical affairs
are all seen to have only the human authority vested in their creation.
When people can really take charge of their distress emotions, then they
may cease to displace them into forms of religious oppression.

## Catharsis and transmutation

But as well as catharsis of distress, the art of suffering includes also the
transmutation of distress emotion - refining the base metal of human
agitation into the gold of comprehensive prescience. Consciousness
training, the management of attention and awareness, the expansion of
mind, the invocation of subtle transmutative energies, prayer, centreing:
all these and more, are part of a practical inquiry into ways of transforming the raw pain of human experience into a new and different
state of mind. Such inquiry is at the interface of person-centred and
transpersonal psychologies, and peer experiential research is best for
dealing with it. It seems that catharsis and transmutation constitute a
necessary dipolar approach to human distress: and we need to know a
great deal more about their interdependence. These are two ways in
which an unseen reality moves in the resolution of human suffering.

## Sources of human stress

Religion has traditionally concerned itself with the management of human suffering and with theoretical accounts of it. In my view it is
doubtful whether either the modes of management or the theories have
been entirely adequate if those originating them did not have a fully
autonomous, human grasp of the many sources of stress which initiate
humans into being and development. For if they did not have this grasp
there is the possibility that unidentified distress would displace into and
distort both the modes of management and the theories.

A comprehensive account of sources of human stress might look something like this:

- Foetal experience and the primal experiences approaching, during
  and after birth.

- The frustration of and interference with physical and psychological
  needs in early infancy and childhood, with residual life-long effects.

- The frustration of and interference with physical and psychological needs in present time, in adulthood.

- Conflicts arising within the interpretation and expression of a given or adopted social role; and between different social roles a person has.

- Constraints due to oppressive organizational structures and procedures (from the family, through the work organization, to the state).

- Constraints due to the oppressive rigidity of prevailing values and norms in the culture and sub-culture to which a person belongs.

Stress to do with certain basic features of the human condition that interact with all the above items:

- The phenomenon of human separation: through birth, partings, death.

- The tension between survival needs and needs for personal and cultural fulfilment.

- Ignorance, lack of knowledge: the apparent inscrutability of many phenomena.

- The intractability of matter and the world; the frustrating gap between ideal and actuality, between vision and its realization.

- The inherent instability of each human being with her or his vast but unprogrammed potential; tension and stress due to the very plethora of choice and possibility for each person.

- The presence of other persons subject to the stresses of all the same conditions.

- Pressures, interferences and constraints due to the unseen climate, to what is going on in the other reality and its incursions into the human realm.

- Being eccentric, off centre, alienated and dissociated from one's Source and Origin.

Authentic personal power, developing individual autonomy, would mean taking charge of these many sources of stress by the use of appropriate resources and strategies. Some are personal growth strategies: to do with regression and catharsis; to do with integration and reprogramming of the personality; to do with interpersonal skills training; to do with life-planning and life-style management; to do with creative expression and expressive style. Some are transpersonal growth strategies: to do with consciousness training and consciousness expansion, with prayer, worship and meditation, with the cultivation of specific forms of access to the other reality. Some are general or job-related education and learning strategies. Some are change agent strategies: to do with organizational development, with creating alternative institutions, with political processes of decision-making wherever decisions are to be made, with social confrontation of the rigid society. Some are technological and ecological strategies. Some are professional, occupational, job-related strategies. And so on. I believe an authentic religion can flourish when it is rooted in the sort of personal power and autonomy generated by this array of competencies.

**Personal and political power**

Particularly important for such authentic religion is the interaction between personal power and political power. Political power is to do with who makes decisions about what. Above all it is to do with whether these decisions are taken over persons and for persons with no consultation with those who are affected by them; or whether they are made with persons, in consultation and collaboration with those affected by them. Participation, co-operation, peer process in decision-making would seem to be the valid political model for a religious organization rooted in the autonomy of persons.

Patriarchy, in which human distress acts out the myth of male supremacy through traditional theology and religious convention, through a whole range of political and social structures, is in my view an anti-religious stance. Androgyny in the psyche, equipotentiality of religious and other roles for both sexes, are further requirements for the religion that affirms personal autonomy. What is important is that there is no sex discrimination in relation to roles that carry charismatic power, political power or both.

---

Perspective 15 is adapted from Chapter 4 in *Paradigm Papers* (Heron, 1981a).

# 16 Living spirit: our process in this place

This Perspective is the revised and enlarged text of a keynote talk I gave on 24 July 2002 at the International Conference on Organizational Spirituality, sponsored by the Human Potential Research Group, which I founded in 1970, at the University of Surrey in the UK. The theme of the conference was *Living Spirit – New Dimensions in Work and Learning*.

## Alternative education

I am a great believer in alternative education and research centres, and I have been involved with others in founding quite a number of them in my time: New Paradigm Research Group; Association of Humanistic Psychology Practitioners; Co-counselling International; Institute for the Development of Human Potential; International Centre for Co-operative Inquiry; South Pacific Centre for Human Inquiry. Even within academic institutions the centres I established were strongly countercultural. The Human Potential Research Project here at the University of Surrey, and the Education Department, and the Research Council for Complementary Medicine, of the British Postgraduate Medical Federation at the University of London, were radically alternative in ideology and methodology.

## Living spirit in educational theory

David Peat, the physicist and polymath, was a neighbour of mine in Italy. He wrote an adventurous book on Blackfoot physics funded by the Fetzer Foundation, also an important biography of David Bohm (Peat, 1996, 1997). Peat had an online discussion group with a number of senior people in science and art. One of the topics that came up was whether established academic institutions were places where significant radical change - toward what truly constitutes the generation of human knowledge and learning - can really occur. It was strongly suggested that alternative institutions will play a vital role in empowering this kind of change. It was an interesting debate and I contributed to it, particularly about one of the big issues, to wit, that established academic institutions - with the exception of an honourable minority - have an inveterate attachment to the unilateral assessment of undergraduate and postgraduate students. Such institutions claim that it is their job, their duty and right, to assess unilaterally whether students have acquired proper and adequate knowledge. In other words, students do not participate in the assessing process: their work is judged entirely from without.

Now I think this kind of unilateral assessment does several things. It certainly keeps control over a sea of anxious students, who are seeking to conform to institutional norms of valid knowledge in order to get their degrees. It certainly exempts staff from any acquiring any of the wide-ranging interpersonal skills required for educating whole persons. Above all, it keeps in a socially dominant place the Aristotelian account of human nature, on the basis of which universities were founded in the Middle Ages: intellectual excellence, theoretical and applied, is the highest end of man (but not woman, according to Aristotle). By and large universities still sustain that model, with the inclusion of women. They are about intellectual excellence in the pursuit of knowledge, and the secondary and incidental function of the intellect is to control and keep in order our emotions and interpersonal behaviour. Students are left to sort out all those supposedly subordinate domains in an *ad hoc* way in their extracurricular activities.

This is not to decry the extraordinary achievement of tertiary institutions of learning since the Middle Ages. But unilateral assessment, and intellectual excellence as the supreme educational goal, tend to perpetuate each other.  Unilaterally assessing students looks much more acceptable and persuasive if you're dealing with purely intellectual propositional work. However, while it seems to be plausible here, I do not think it really is.

In a comprehensive model of learning, three things go together and are to be practised concurrently: learning the content of a discipline; learning how to learn; and learning to assess how well you have learned. This means a significant element of student self-direction in choosing content and learning methods, through setting up learning contracts in collaboration with staff. Also a significant element of student self-assessment in choosing criteria of assessment and applying them, also in collaboration with staff. Staff as culture-carriers need to pass on to their students not merely the content of knowledge, but a progressively developing proficiency in self-directed learning and self-directed assessment of that learning (Heron, 1988).

A comprehensive model of learning further includes the application of an extended epistemology. This means integrating into the learning process at least four basic ways of knowing, not just the one intellectual/conceptual/propositional way. First we have experiential knowing: by meeting/encounter/engagement with people, places, processes and things – that is, by participation in the being of what is present – a process which I regard as fundamentally spiritual, and as the ground of the next three. Second there is presentational knowing: by intuitive grasp of the meaning of the patterns and forms of nonverbal imagery, as in the various arts, in immediate perceiving, in memory and dreams. Third we have our very familiar propositional, conceptual knowing, mediated by language. And fourth there's practical knowing: knowing how to do things, manifest in a whole array of skills and competencies – spiritual, psychic, aesthetic, intellectual, political, interpersonal, emotional, technical, clinical, and so on.

There is more, for a comprehensive model of learning is integral, holistic. This means the four ways of knowing and learning are mutually supportive and enhancing: the soundness of each one is interdependent with the soundness of the other three. So the quality of your intellectual learning is affected by the quality of your engagement with people, places and nature; by the quality of your grasp of the significance of nonverbal imagery, in perception, memory, imagination, visions, dreams, and your artistic productions; by the quality of your know-how, your skills in diverse areas of internal and external life. Thus your intellectual education is a manifest of your personal, interpersonal, ecological and practical growth, grounded in your open participation in the being of what is present (Heron, 1992, 1996a, 1996b, 1999).

This integral account of learning puts an end to the Aristotelian doctrine of intellectual excellence as the supreme educational end. For it suggests that the primary outcomes of education are transformations of your being-in-connectedness - essentially the unfoldment of indwelling spirit - and the range of competencies and skills which manifest this. And that the presentational and propositional outcomes of education are grounded in those more fundamental kinds of change. Within this integral model, it becomes morally and spiritually dubious to suppose that you can unilaterally assess someone else's personal-spiritual development as a ground for their presentational and propositional learning. For it is at the heart of this kind of development that what authenticates it is a spiritual authority that lies deep within each person. Indeed if staff run a course that requires a certain amount of spiritual development, and unilaterally assess students' spiritual outcomes, with the possibility of spiritually failing people, then they have simply re-created a contemporary version of the inquisition. Assessment in such a course can only properly be collaborative with staff, with a strong component of student self-assessment.

So unilateral assessment becomes profoundly problematic when you get into the deeper reaches of human nature and incorporate them into the whole learning process. I don't know whether universities and other tertiary institutions are going to rise to the challenge of truly integral learning and survive - because of their inability to relinquish their final unilateral dominance, their absolute power to control the knowledge market. Their capitalization of knowledge says "We are the people who know who knows: we say who has got the knowledge and who has not". And it is precisely this kind of capitalization which is rendered obsolete by the alternative centres, which are better called networks, of the emerging peer to peer age.

**Living spirit in peer to peer processes**

For what is irresistibly coming forward, through peer to peer processes, is the democratization of human knowledge – participative collaboration in the generation and dissemination of knowledge – in a way that has never occurred before. It's the outcome of a potent marriage between radical ideology and advances in information technology.

Consider the free software movement, launched by Richard Stallman, which produces software such as GNU and Linux. Tens of thousands of programmers are co-operatively producing the most valuable knowledge capital of the day, software. They are doing this in small groups that are seamlessly co-coordinated in the greater worldwide project, in true peer groups that have no traditional hierarchy. This movement involves four kinds of freedom:

- Freedom to run the program for any purpose.

- Freedom to study how the program works, and to adapt it to your needs (access to the source code is a precondition for this).

- Freedom to redistribute copies so you can help your neighbour.

- Freedom to improve the program and release your improvements to the public, so that the whole community benefits (access to the source code is also a precondition for this).

Consider wireless LANs – local area networks, that could also be called learning area networks. In Hawaii a peer to peer wireless network covers more 300 square miles. It's free: anyone who wants to link up can do so at no charge. All you need is the right equipment and a password.

All over the island people are tapping in: creative collaboration goes on among high school teachers, among wildlife regulators, and others. Similarly in the Bay area of San Francisco there is also an extensive low cost wireless network, used by citizens for all kinds of peer to peer purposes.

In cyberspace information and knowledge can be generated anywhere and made accessible everywhere. Already millions of people are freely producing and exchanging information on the web. This massive amount of informative interaction between random equal citizens is an emerging counter-ballast to market culture of all kinds. As we get more and more overlapping and intermeshed wireless local area networks that are free - in terms of both liberty and cost – and avoid central servers altogether, so that no-one capitalizes on any of it, then the dominant market culture is severely compromised. This is already happening on a very wide scale in the music world with the general public download-ing millions of songs, a process which is untraceable and immune to le-gal challenge with the use of the new peer to peer technology. And in the video world, people are re-editing and freely re-distributing Holly-wood movies, to make them more true to the original story-line (Bau-wens, 2006).

There is a very wealthy Japanese electronics company, doing a 3 trillion yen a year business in mobile phones. They have got a major research centre in silicon valley in California and I had a long talk with the American who runs it. The company is into third generation mobile phones and speculating about fourth generation mobile media devices. They currently dominate their particular market. The bosses in Japan want to keep control of it so that they can continue to make an enor-mous amount of money. The manager of the research centre is, how-ever, very forward thinking. He is telling the bosses that it is no good supposing they can go on with their capitalist control of the market. He is saying that they have got to accept the democratization that is spread-ing rapidly on the web, to face the fact that there will be an increasing number of these peer to peer wireless LANs all over the place; and that the most the company can hope to do is to say to them "Look, if you contract with us we can provide you with expert resources and services that will facilitate your interactive autonomy". He's urging them to humble themselves, and realize that they will only survive if they take account of, and offer specialist services to, the rising tide of peer to peer electronic autonomy-in-co-operation. But the Japanese bosses are not having it: they do not like it, and are having difficulty in hearing it. I think they would be wise to listen attentively.

It is only a matter of time before the prevailing academic marketing of knowledge by tertiary institutions - selling to students institutionally validated knowledge-claims - becomes similarly challenged. Within the next hundred years, the rising tide of peer to peer civilization will surely bypass those who continue to try to control and market valid knowledge. This is a looming threat to all established institutions that insist on the unilateral assessment of students. The crisis is now, but there is little evidence that the academic capitalists are any more alert to the challenge than the electronic capitalists in Japan.

Years ago there used to be a free university in Amsterdam. My daughter participated in it for about a year. This was a group of students practising autonomy-in-connectedness, hiring external staff on a contract basis, so that staff hierarchy was authorized by student autonomy and co-operation. This was a harbinger of things to come, before the birth of the internet.

Now knowledge and information is everywhere accessible, and the signposts are already well marked out. Human beings are spontaneously getting into interconnected networks, which give birth to, and nourish the creative interdependence between, individual autonomy and social co-operation. It's the prescient vision of Kropotkin (1842-1921) starting to manifest sooner than any of us expected: a society of free voluntary associations, spontaneously arising, united within and without by mutual agreements, decentralized and self-governing, awakening the constructive powers of the masses.

It is the grip of a humanly inappropriate degree of control which characterizes the current dominant world order: the control of commodities and services by large corporations; the control of valid knowledge by academic establishments like this and others. It's a sort of control that is out of tune with the emerging civilization, simply not with it. I commend to you the paper by Michel Bauwens (2006) 'Peer to peer and human evolution'. It provides a useful overview of peer to peer developments as technological paradigm on the internet, as distribution mechanism, as production method, in manufacturing, in politics and social change, in spirituality, in knowledge generation.

**Living spirit in the dawn of the age of immanence**

What I believe all this really shows is the newly emerging power of the human spirit, the dawning age of divine immanence, of the indwelling spirit that is the ground of human motivation. I think that living spirit is active within us, the very deep source of all human aspiration, both the will to live as a distinct individual, and the will to live as a universal participant – the will to be one of the creative Many and to be engaged with the creative One. These profound impulses have for the past 3,000 years been predominantly subordinate to the authoritative control of religious traditions, teachers and texts which have promoted spirit as primarily transcendent.

And where these impulses have been emancipated from such control they have been reduced to secular status. Secular modernity has delivered huge gains in terms of relatively autonomous ethics, politics, science, knowledge generally, and art. Yet it has championed the autonomy of the isolated Cartesian ego, separated off from the world it seeks to categorize, codify and manage.

I do think this is the century of the spirit that is living deep within: the self-actualizing tendency of Rogers (1959, 1980), Maslow (1970), Gendlin (1981), embedded within the body-mind; the bio-spiritual experience of grace in the body of McMahon and Campbell (1991); Jean Houston's entelechy self, the ground of one's being, the root self whence all our possibilities emerge (Houston, 1987); Washburn's dynamic ground of libido, psychic energy, numinous power or spirit (Washburn, 1995); Wilber's ground unconscious, Eros, spirit-in-action (Wilber, 2000a).

Instead of appealing to the spiritual authority of teacher, tradition and text, an increasing number of people respond co-creatively with this divine dynamic moving within. Spiritual authority is found in the exercise of a deep kind of inner discrimination, where human autonomy and divine animation marry. Nikolai Berdyaev (1874-1948), in the great tradition of European personalism, with which I align myself, was on to it with his affirmation of human personhood as manifesting the creative process of spirit. For he defined spirit as self-determining human subjectivity engaged in the realization of value and achieved in true community. He used the excellent Russian word *sobornost* to name such a community: it means diversity in free unity. Berdyaev also had a wonderful vision of the impending era, which he called the third epoch. The third epoch is the epoch of divine-human co-creation of a transformed planet, transformed persons, transformed social relationships (Berdyaev, 1937).

Translated into my conceptual system, Berdyaev's account means that living spirit manifests as a dynamic interplay between autonomy, hierarchy and co-operation. It emerges through autonomous people each of whom who can identify their own idiosyncratic true needs and interests; each of whom can also think hierarchically in terms of what values promote the true needs and interests of the whole community; and each of whom can co-operate with – that is, listen to, engage with, and negotiate agreed decisions with - their peers, celebrating diversity and difference as integral to genuine unity.

Hierarchy here is the creative leadership which seeks to promote the values of autonomy and co-operation in a peer to peer association. Such leadership, as in the free software movement mentioned earlier, is exercised in two ways.

- First, by the one or more people who take initiatives to set up such an association.

- Second, once the association is up and running, as spontaneous rotating leadership among the peers, when anyone takes initiatives that further enhance the autonomy and co-operation of other participating members.

The autonomy of participants is not that of the old Cartesian ego, isolated and cut off from the world. Descartes sat inside a big stove to get at his *cogito, ergo sum* - I think, therefore I am – and while his exclusively subjective self provided a necessary leverage against traditional dogmatisms to help found the modern worldview, it left the modern self alienated from the separated world it commands.

The autonomy of those who flourish within *sobornost*, by contrast, is an autonomy that is rounded and enriched by a profound kind of inner animation, that develops and flourishes only in felt interconnectedness, participative engagement, with other persons, and with the biodiversity and integral ecology of our planet (Spretnak, 1995).

This is the participatory worldview, expressed also in the extended epistemology I mentioned earlier on: our conceptual knowing of the world is grounded in our experiential knowing – a felt resonance with the world and imaginal participation in it. This epistemic participation is the ground for political participation in social processes that integrate autonomy, hierarchy and co-operation. What we are now about is a whole collaborative regeneration of our world through co-creative engagement with the spirit that animates it and us. For just a few of the many contributors to the participatory worldview see: Abram, 1996; Bateson, 1979; Berman, 1981; Ferrer, 2002; Heron, 1992, 1996a, 1998; Merleau-Ponty, 1962; Skolimowski, 1994; Spretnak, 1991; Reason, 1994; Reason and Rowan, 1981; Tarnas, 1991; Varela, Thompson and Rosch, 1991.

## Living spirit in educational practice

As I said earlier, I'm certainly a great believer in alternative education and research, both without and within established institutions. So here are some of my modest attempts to work with living spirit, with two examples from within the establishment, and one from without. I started the Human Potential Research Project (HPRP) at this university in November 1970. I set it up as an autonomous entity within the Centre for Adult Education - which at that time was an extramural department.

The HPRP had a purely extramural focus. As a matter of political prudence, in those early days, we made no attempt to attract intramural undergraduate or postgraduate students, but if they happened to get wind of us and turned up for our workshops, they were welcome. So our publicity went exclusively to the general public and professional groups in the surrounding community. Through the first year I ran a programme of weekend Human Relations Training Laboratories.

I facilitated the unfolding dynamic of each experiential group based on a few simple and basic ground-rules to which everyone had assented. The idea was that participants would acquire new intrapsychic and interpersonal awareness, insights and skills. My guiding definition of love, for professional facilitators and helpers, was "to provide conditions within which people can in liberty determine their own true needs and interests in co-operation with others who are similarly engaged". It's a definition which again points to the interdependence of autonomy and co-operation, facilitated by the hierarchy of a benign facilitation which reminds people of the full implications of the ground-rules to which they have agreed. This approach to empowering facilitation gradually evolved into a comprehensive facilitator training format (Heron, 1999).

So that was the underlying approach behind that first year of experiential learning. The next year, I added a twenty week, one evening a week, co-counselling training course. Co-counselling is a form of peer self-help psychotherapy, a peer-to-peer alternative mental health network. Over the next three years we developed it at the HPRP in direction that led to a break with the originating authoritarian organization in the USA, and we and colleagues in the USA set up the entirely independent organization of Co-counselling International, in which hierarchical roles are solely validated by their effectiveness in bringing viable peer-to-peer communities into being. These communities now exist in a peer-to-peer federal format spanning many countries in the world.

I ran that first co-counselling course as an experiential inquiry (Heron, 1971), a precursor of co-operative inquiry. which was in fact implicit in a diversity of workshops run at the HPRP in through the 1970s. It became fully explicit as a peer-to-peer alternative research method in 1981 (Heron, 1981b).

In the third year, I started working with the medical profession, training experienced GPs to become trainers of young hospital doctors entering General Practice. When the senior GP course-organizers first approached me about a course, I said they should only work with me if they were interested in my educational model: the programme would be co-designed by the organizers, the participants and myself, negotiating to include our various concerns and interests; and that my concerns included not only this participative decision-making, but also a significant element of experiential learning using structured exercises of various kinds. They nervously agreed to the model. The course took off and became powerful experiential learning arena, especially through the use of role play to differentiate between facilitative (you tell me) and authoritative (I tell you) interventions in the GPs' relations both with their trainees and with their patients. In those days most of the GPs couldn't really tell the difference: every initial attempt to be facilitative got compulsively skewed into an authoritative form (e.g. "Don't you think that what you really ought to do with this patient is…").

Those courses went on for some time and were a great success, a breakthrough in medical education. As a result, after seven years with the Project at Surrey, I was head-hunted by the British Postgraduate Medical Federation (BPMF) of the University of London for an extremely anomalous appointment as Assistant Director to organize, run and innovate within, their Education Department. It was anomalous because it was unprecedented for someone with no medical background to fill such a senior position at the top of the academic medical hierarchy. I realized that this was an extremely hazardous prospect. I accepted the post on condition that I could write my own job-description, with signed assent to it from the Federation. This was to be my contractual protection, because I knew that once I started to innovate, all hell would break loose.

So the Education Department within the BPMF was, like the Human Potential Research Project within the University of Surrey, an alternative education and research centre. The program of courses I put on was so radical, by conventional medical education standards, that some non-participant doctors were outraged. But a high percentage of the participating doctors were liberated into new vistas of thought and practice, and medically empowered in a patient-centred way (Heron, 1984). The courses had interrelated themes: medical education as the facilitation of whole person learning; medical practice as the facilitation of whole person healing; emotional competence and interpersonal skills in relating to patients/staff/colleagues; in-depth personal development as a foundation for professional development; revision of the ethical and philosophical assumptions on which modern medicine is based.

After the first few years at the BPMF, I launched a co-operative inquiry – and by then the method was fully developed - into whole person medicine for sixteen experienced GPs. This ran for nine months and we met every six weeks for a long weekend to review and reflect on the innovations of medical practice applied in the previous weeks (Heron and Reason, 1985). Prior to this there was a preliminary weekend at which we worked out a provisional model of whole person medicine. It included a statement about the integration of body, mind and spirit. When it came to planning the third six-week action cycle, one subgroup said "Look, our model includes this idea of integrating body-mind-spirit, but what does this mean in practice in the NHS in our consulting room?". So they contracted to try out different sorts of spiritual intervention for six weeks and review and revise them at the subsequent reflection weekend. Another sub-group elected to look at power-sharing with patients. This, it seemed to me, was also another way of engaging with living spirit. It was fascinating the things both sub-groups tried out. It was indeed living spirit at work. Some doctors found that if, at an appropriate time in the consultation, they could just pop in a simple question like "What do you think about prayer?" or "When you're ill where does religion figure in the experience?", then a new depth of authentic relationship and healing potential could be opened up. A doctor once asked a patient of the Islamic faith about prayer and found out that this man spent so many times a day down on his knees praying, that extra light was thrown on the aetiology of his presenting knee problem. Patrick Pietroni and some of the other doctors participating in our inquiry went on to found the British Holistic Medical Association.

Now both these alternative education centres, within the universities of Surrey and London, offered no university diplomas, certificates or degrees for any of their courses. I chose this as a matter of deliberate policy, for both universities would have insisted on unilateral assessment as a non-negotiable precondition for granting any university qualification. And such assessment was incompatible with the kind of in-depth whole-person education which these centres practised. So in 1977, in London, five of us founded the entirely independent Institute for the

Development of Human Potential (IDHP), to run two-year part-time courses, integrating experiential and theoretical learning, and offering a Diploma in Humanistic Psychology, awarded on the basis of the rigorous practice of self and peer assessment by students trained in the method throughout the course by the course facilitators.

This institute was launched by the initiative of David Blagden Marks, the second director of Quaesitor, the first growth centre in London, indeed in Europe. A year after the launch, David, a single-handed transatlantic yachtsman, was tragically drowned in a severe storm when crossing the Irish sea, after setting sail on the basis of a highly inaccurate weather report. As we reeled from this tragedy, I took the rudder and became chairperson of the IDHP for a period as we refined our educational ideology and method. The IDHP is still going strong, with current courses in process, and its twenty five years of educational pioneering were celebrated by four articles in *Self and Society* in 2001 (vol. 29, no. 2, June-July). It has consistently affirmed, among other things, the following: experiential learning, in the spirit of inquiry, as the ground of multi-faceted integral learning – personal, interpersonal, political, spiritual; emotional competence as a prerequisite for facilitative skills (the interdependence of personal and professional development); the intentional and empowering interplay of hierarchy, co-operation and autonomy in the relation between facilitators and participants, and in the unfolding of course dynamics; the application of self and peer assessment as the sole basis of accreditation.

What is so important about self and peer assessment and using it as a basis for diploma accreditation, is that it affirms to society at large that the validating authority for personal-cum-professional-cum-spiritual development lies primarily within the depths of each individual person, where that person is profoundly engaged with other persons in the developmental process and where that person is within an educational culture that promotes the cultivation of integral learning and self and peer assessment skills. Autonomous self-assessment is set in a context of rigorous peer assessment and institutional training. The autonomy is interdependent with peer process and institutional hierarchy. This interacting triad of autonomy, co-operation and hierarchy (Heron, 1999) is a theme that runs through my whole talk, and is, perhaps, a key to the dynamics of the emerging peer to peer world.

**Living spirit in terms of a broad map of participatory spirituality**

Spiritual development fully considered is, in my view, the same thing as participatory action inquiry into the immanent depths, the transcendent heights and the situational immediacy of the human condition. And in this total arena, pre-eminently, the ultimate authority is within. Benjamin Whichcote (1609-1683), the Cambridge Platonist, got it precisely right when he said, "If you have a revelation from God, I must have a revelation from God too before I can believe you".

Once the impeccable spiritual logic of that statement is grasped, then it is clear that the external authority of a teacher, a text, or a tradition rests on a prior internal authority, projected outward. And once such projection is fully withdrawn, then we may have peer dialogue with teacher, tradition and text – as co-inquirers - but we never surrender to them. Final spiritual authority rests in that extraordinary interaction between inner divinity and personal autonomy. And this in wise dialogue with our peers, so that we can refine both our critical subjectivity and critical intersubjectivity (Heron, 1998).

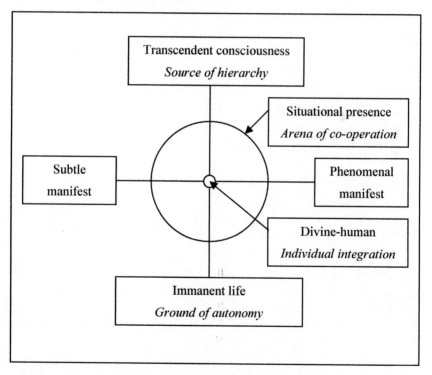

*Figure 5: divine-human integration (repeat of Figure 3)*

These comments set the scene for having a look at the little map (figure above) which is projected on the screen here, and which I currently use for my own personal spiritual inquiries. I also use it for the launch of what I call experiential journeys of opening, before a co-operative inquiry into the spiritual and the subtle. This map is a provisional template, it carries no external authority, it is just an authentic adventure in my mind. Do not project and hide your own internal authority within it.

This whole thing is a model of the divine. I differentiate between the divine, which is everything on this map taken together, and spirit - which is the bipolar vertical line. At one end of this line is spirit as transcendent consciousness: the unborn, the uncreate, beyond all name and form, beyond all manifestation. At the other end is spirit as immanent life: the radical ground of our autonomy and motivation, indwelling animation, the divine impulse within, primal shakti, the ultimate root of our will to live as an individual and our will to live as a universal participant.

Here the horizontal line is creation, the realm of manifestation. At one end is the phenomenal manifest, by which I simply mean the visible universe, nature and society. At the other end is the subtle manifest: parallel and complementary realities - what you see opening out at the end of the tunnel in a near death experience, the realms Monroe visited in his out of the body experiences (Monroe, 1972), what Siegfried Sassoon portrayed in his evocative poem:

> I looked on that prophetic land
> Where manifested by their powers
> Presences perfected stand
> Whom might and day no more command
> With shine and shadow of earthly hours.

> I saw them, numberless they stood
> Halfway toward heaven, that man might mark
> The grandeur of their ghostlihood
> Burning divinely in the dark.

Indigenous cultures know all about the realm of the ancestors and its relevance to every day life. In New Zealand there is still an extant Maori culture aware of this relevance; and a discriminating minority of the pakeha (European settler) population are learning to understand there is something important going on there.

The circle on the map is, for anyone contemplating it, his or her immediate present social and physical situation. So for us here, it is our process in this place. From my perspective, this circle of a person's present social and physical location is the primary locus of human spirituality. The circle, indeed, is local divinity, the integration of the spiritual and the manifest here in this situation where we are. This means that relational forms of spiritual practice, to do with the relation between persons and the immediate environment, and between persons present in the situation, are fundamental, central. Purely inward and individualistic forms of spiritual practice, such as certain kinds of meditation, are, I believe, secondary and supportive.

Many traditional forms of spiritual practice are inward and individualistic, concerned with opening to spirit as transcendent consciousness. They are a splendid legacy of the spiritual traditions of the past three thousand years, whose theologies have been focused first and foremost on spirit as transcendent. They will have a life forever. But to continue today to make these practices the *primary* route to spirit is, for me, a misplaced allegiance to the spiritual values of a rapidly receding era. All on their own, they tend to have two effects: firstly, to inflate the local divinity of our process in this place to absolute divinity, that is, to inflate the human view to the God's eye view; and secondly and relatedly, to lead to inappropriate authoritarianism in the political management of spiritual community and of spiritual education and training.

|  | **Immanent life** | **Situational presence** | **Transcendent consciousness** |
|---|---|---|---|
| Opening | Wellspring evocation<br><br>Charismatic opening | Feeling presence<br><br>Seamless perceiving | Lens of attention<br><br>Transcendental subjectivity |
| Acting | Life-style choices<br><br>Primary theatre & lean ritual | Participatory decision-making<br><br>Life-style transformation | Refracting powers & presences<br><br>Illuminated language |
|  | *Enlivenment* | *Engagement* | *Enlightenment* |

Figure 6: the three ways (repeat of Figure 4)

My map suggests there are three interdependent divine ways: the way of engagement, the way of enlivenment, and the way of enlightenment – three interacting modes of integral practice (figure above). Each way involves the polar dynamic of opening up, and manifesting in action; and the manifesting, I believe, consummates the opening up. First, there is the way of engagement with situational presence, with the divine evident here and now as our process in this place. This means opening to the spirit of relationship in this situation, opening to the reality that connects. "Only connect" wrote the novelist E.M.Forster.

The root practice of this engagement simply exercises our innate capacity for feeling the presence of places, people and other entities and processes. Through this capacity of the spiritual heart we enter directly into a sense of interconnectedness with the presences in our world. We feel communion, resonance, attunement, the reality of the go-between spirit in the mutuality of relationship. Correlative with this is the practice of opening to the seamless process of perceiving: noticing that there is no gap between seer, seeing and seen; between hearer, hearing and heard; between toucher, touching and touched; between us, the world we image in any sensory, and extrasensory, mode and the imaging process.

To perceive a world is to feel, to participate in, an ongoing interfusion of our being and other beings, through sensory and extrasensory imaging, an interfusion which reveals the distinctness of each within the interactive communion and mutual enfolding of all, and which is also enriched, enhanced and extended by practices on the way of enlivenment and the way of enlightenment.

The business of communion and seamless perceiving is not something to be constructed and manufactured. It is more a matter of uncovering and noticing what is already going on as an innate condition  of our being-in-a-world. We open fully and equally to inner and outer experiences, while letting go of any tight conceptual grip upon them, and at the same time abandoning any compulsive emotional grasp of them. Then we enjoy their seamless marriage within the circumambient embrace of being.

When it comes to action on the way of engagement, the great adventure is that of participatory decision-making, which integrates autonomy, co-operation and hierarchy: people co-operating in groups discussing and deciding actions to transform their personhood, their society and their planet. In this practice, each person moves between and integrates three positions: autonomy – being clear what I genuinely need, want and wish for, what my idiosyncratic preferences are, in relation to the matter being discussed; hierarchy - thinking on behalf of the whole group and the wider community within which the action will be embedded; and co-operation – listening to, empathising with, and negotiating agreed decisions with, my peers, decisions that integrate diversity, difference and unity.

I think this process manifests living spirit. It is a profound spiritual practice: exhilarating, liberating, and challenging participants with the discomforts of ego-burning. There may be a lot of ego-burning early on in the history of a peer to peer group, and then a co-operative dynamic emerges, incorporating an elegantly and spontaneously rotating hierarchy or leadership. In this dynamic, there is a period of sharing of idiosyncratic autonomous needs, interests and viewpoints, then one person comes up with an integral proposal that resonates strongly with the group. This process continues on with the hierarchical luminosity moving around to different people, each of whom sheds practical integral light on the preceding chunk of autonomous-co-operative discussion.

It seems wise to allow for periods of a greater or lesser proximity to chaos and confusion. The strongest version of this idea comes from complexity theory, which asserts that complex systems need to get to the edge of chaos as a necessary precursor to re-integrating at new levels of order. At this edge, fixed assumptions are rattled, ego burns up; then a new order dawns. If a group doesn't deconstruct sufficiently, it won't reconstruct in a fresh space of learning and awareness. This applies to radical inquiry groups, rather than to everyday management groups. However, while it is a plausible principle, I wouldn't want to make too much of a rule of it in any context.

What is clear is that the kind of sophisticated spiritual skill in participatory decision-making, which I have outlined, has a huge claim for attention on our planet. And many precursors are afoot. There is co-operative inquiry (Heron, 1996a), and related forms of participatory action research going on in various parts of the world (e.g. Reason and Bradbury, 2001; Reason, 2002; Yorks and Kasl, 2002). There is the peer spirit circling of Christina Baldwin and Ann Linnea, based near Seattle, and affirmed by them as a spiritual practice (Baldwin and Linnea, 2000). This is a fine model of the integration of autonomy, co-operation and hierarchy in group discussion and decision-making, and is being practised in many different contexts in the USA. The Green Party of Utah (2002) have put out a useful account of consensus collaborative decision-making, and make the point that the process, the practice, is as important as its outcomes. And there is, of course, a great deal more.

To return now to three divine ways suggested on my map. Second, there is the way of enlivenment, opening up to and manifesting immanent spiritual life, divine animation moving the bodymind and all creation. The associated spiritual practices, which we have explored through co-operative inquiry both in the centre in Italy and now in New Zealand, are charismatic opening and primary theatre. Charismatic opening is the simple and radical process of opening up the bodymind and its primary energies - through improvised gesture, posture, alignment, movement, rhythm, vocal sound and declaration - to the indwelling empowering presence of divine animation. This can be experienced as an all-consuming, all-sustaining, all-creating everywhere active experiential fire.

Primary theatre extends charismatic opening to respond creatively to the promptings of indwelling life, giving dynamic form and voice to one's immediate relation with what there is; to explore, reveal and affirm in nonverbal and verbal ways one's primary, original relation with creation. I have written about primary theatre in Chapter 8 of the fifth edition of *Helping the Client* (2001b); and about charismatic opening in Chapter 12 of *The Complete Facilitator's Handbook* (1999) – which also describes in detail its application to facilitation as a relational form of spiritual practice. And this application, together with its extension into all sorts of other social roles, manifests charismatic enlivenment in daily action.

Third, there is the way of enlightenment, which does not mean here a path to any final end-state, just an ongoing practice calling for integration with the other two ways. This practice opens to transcendent consciousness: we disidentify from any kind of manifest form into uncreated, unborn spirit beyond all differentiation - the simple, liberated space of awareness. I find that this liberated space eventually always gently and warmly disavows the disidentification and settles down around the cosmic and psychological content which it both includes and transcends. A classic Tibetan practice is attending to everyday awareness as such and opening to its intrinsic continuity with the free attention of the universe, the great crystal mirror of cosmic mind within which all things are reflected (Govinda, 1960). A related practice, championed by Ramana Maharshi on his sacred hill in south India, is opening to transcendental subjectivity, inquiring inwardly into the origin of one's everyday 'I' and finding it's source in the all-encompassing divine 'I am' (Gangaji, 1995). It is interesting to note that transcendent practice can be integrated with the immanent practice of charismatic opening and its application in seamless perceiving. This yields their potent dynamic unity within the situational present (see Figure 6).

The model of spirit in my map is bipolar: there is influence upward from immanent life, divine animation; there is influence downward from transcendent consciousness, divine mind. But the relation between the up-hierarchy and the down-hierarchy is one of parity. They are interdependent - mutually fructifying in a marriage of differentiated equals. And the site of their marriage, with each other and with the manifest realms, is the situational present, our process in this place. It seems to me that human collegiality is the consummation of this marriage: persons in dynamic co-creative relation with each other, with divine animation and divine awareness, integrating autonomy, co-operation and hierarchy in transforming their way of being in their interrelated sensory and subtle worlds.

## Questions and answers

M (Member of audience). A lot of my learning has come out of a model which you're going away from, the guru model, where there's a figure of great authority and personal attainment, such as Ramana Maharshi. I left that model because it felt the right thing to do, and I've been more involved in the collaborative side of things that you're suggesting. Yet somehow I still haven't quite found the edge of learning or the power of learning that I found before. But I don't want to go back to what I was using before, or in any way instigate that kind of thing myself. Does that ring any bells?

J (John Heron). Can you refine the question?

M. The question is this: Is there a danger of the kind of flat land where some sort of quality is lost?

J. A sharp answer is: Only if you keep projecting it out somewhere. If it's flat land and you feel there's no qualitative authority around, then in my view that means there's still some residual unprocessed projection on to past authority figures. If you look at my book, *Sacred Science,* I explore the notion of projecting spiritual authority outward in different ways at different stages (Heron, 1998). The guru tradition fostered this projection and made a virtue of it – the guru is your Self – and this has indeed powerfully enabled a certain kind of spiritual development on the way of transcendence. In fact, historically, in the long age of transcendent religions, now fading, almost all spiritual development of the human race has been a function of projecting authority onto tradition, teacher and text. Today, however, I think we're at a cross-over stage, learning to withdraw the projections and ground own our autonomous authority within the way of immanence. It's partly to do with a dynamic paradox of the information age. It provokes all sorts of spiritual teachers to get out there and claim their market share of projections. But the more authoritative teachers there are, the more it becomes obvious to the seeker, first, that he or she needs to exercise great inner discrimination in choosing between them all; and then, of course, that this very inner discrimination is precisely where the true guidance, splendour and luminosity lies. It seems to me that if your projection is only partially withdrawn, then of course it's not a flat land out there, it's a no mans land. So check in and see whether you're still harbouring a hidden residue of strong spiritual projection. How can it be flat land, how can it be no mans land, how *can* it be - unless I've prostrated myself into a flat position?

M.  I find what you are proposing to us, what you are reporting to us, is a process we're already engaged in very loosely. My question is actually similar to the previous question. Where in all this is the discipline of development? Is it the discipline you've described for group transformation, in a way the opening of the heart of the group, rather than bringing through the paramount clarity of spirit?

J.  Look, it's wonderful stuff, but don't let's be too fooled by the 'paramount clarity of spirit' of luminous teachers within the transcendent traditions. Even Wilber acknowledges that there can be 'nondual sufficiency which leaves schmucks as it finds them' and the 'stone Buddha' practitioner, proficient in sustaining formless awareness through discipline and attention to the guru, but whose emotional, interpersonal and sexual life is just a mess (Wilber, 2000b). Take the brilliant Tibetan Buddhist tulku Kali Rinpoche, much renowned in Europe. In his later years he took to himself a secret sexual consort, a young Scottish woman of 22, June Campbell. Now middle-aged, she has after many years come out about this past relationship in her book *Traveler in Space*, and about the persistent role of misogyny in sustaining monastic patriarchy (Campbell, 1996). The tulku presented himself to his followers as celibate throughout the sexual relationship with Campbell, which he in no way publicly acknowledged. When she protested that maybe they could be open about it, an aide told her that in a previous incarnation his holiness had also had a consort who made a similar complaint, whereupon he cast a spell upon her and she died.

Buddhist mysticism is in many ways magnificent, I've learnt a huge amount from it. But if you look at the attitude of traditional Buddhist mystics they both want the divine female principle in their theology and mystical symbolism, but the human woman they abuse and treat like trash, as Campbell makes clear. It's an unbelievable degree of dissonance and hypocrisy.

When the brilliant Tibetan teacher C. Trungpa first came to Europe, to a community in the north of England, he bedded and wedded a sixteen year old woman. He was found drunk, lying prone on the bathroom floor, intoning mantras into the tiles. So they kicked him out and he went on to the USA, where set up the famed Shambhala institute. There he died of alcoholic poisoning at the age of 47. His immediate successor died of AIDS, having infected several other members of the spiritual community.

The dramatic spread of Zen and Tibetan institutions in the USA has led in many sad cases to the sexual exploitation of young followers of both genders and severe financial irregularity, with no proper accountability, and both western and oriental teachers were involved (Crook, 1996). So there's been a massive abuse of spiritual projection within these kinds of hierarchical spirituality. In the same way, the lid has come off the Catholic Church. Let's take the lid off all these things. Don't be fooled by the august nature of the holiness.

The relational forms of spiritual practice don't appear, at first blush, to be spiritual simply because of a long habituated cultural addiction to misplaced transcendence. But once you get into them your realize their elegance and sweet profundity. My partner Barbara and I, we do a variety of relational forms of spiritual practice. Let me share one that we use pretty much every day, and have used over many years. It's one of the most fundamental, and it's about the way we make decisions on a huge range of issues, large and small, that affect both our needs and interests. We each decide first in private, without telling each other, what our individual autonomous preferences are. So we train and discipline ourselves to notice where we really stand on any issue, to uncover hidden and subtle preferences, as well as own very obvious ones. Then we disclose these preferences to each other, so we can co-operate in reaching a decision as autonomous individuals. If the preferences are quite different, then one or the other or both of us will find the creative hierarchical position and come up with an integral third proposal that motivates us both. This practice is rigorous, it's a well-honed discipline. It's also always interesting, because we are continually learning about each other; and it's often a lot of fun.

There's a huge creative rigour and excitement in relational forms of spiritual practice and at this early stage in the peer to peer age, we know only a small number of them. There is a great call in the heart to open up to them. I sometimes get up in the hours before dawn and sit in a LAZ-E-BOY chair and engage in one of the most individualistic kinds of traditional practice, opening up to transcendent formless awareness. After an hour so I notice that it descends gently into the heart, waiting for social action.

M. I've found what you've said very inspiring especially, and I've heard a lot of what we've done in these three days and with Anita Roddick last night in particular, as a kind of wave call. In the beginning Josie said let's consider this as a learning community, and I'm very much hearing that in what you've said. Everything we need is here in this room and this group of people coming together can achieve something beyond our greatest imaginings. Do you have any advice or suggestions?

J. My advice is coded into my encouragement of peer to peer processes: co-operate with, and/or receive support from, peers in autonomous networks, to create alternative centres of excellence within whatever established institutions you work. Established institutions are porous, there are many apertures within their apparently rigid institutional grids. And the apertures are hungry to have flowers planted in them.

Let me just quickly tell you how I founded the Human Potential Research Project here. Believe it or not, it was because of seven senior police officers: they started it off. In the late summer of 1970, the Assistant Chief Constable of Surrey Police, who was also in charge of training, rang the Vice-Chancellor's office and said: "Could you please set up a course for seven of my senior police officers, to improve relations between town and gown". That office got in touch with David James, the head of the Adult Education Centre, and asked him to put on a five day course. David went into shock, got in touch with me and said: "Could you run the first two days, I know you're doing lectures for the Royal Institute of Public Administration?" I agreed to do it. After my two days, there was to be a day with the sociologists, then two final days with the computing unit, as I recall. Seven worldly-wise, professionally competent, senior police officers of Superintendent rank came through the door of one of the smaller teaching rooms in the lecture theatre block, on a Monday morning. I said to them: "Look, I can give you two days of lectures. But I could also do something else, which will require courage from all of us: courage from me because I've never done it before with people of your professional standing; courage from you because it's an invitation for you to explore the relation between your humanity and your professional role, through a series of simple but radical exercises, and to take some risks in the presence of your peers". As soon as they heard the word 'courage' they lined up on the edge of the pool ready to plunge in at the deep end and we were off. We had an extraordinary two day journey. They looked at what motivated them to join the police in the first place, and at what motivated them in the job today. They explored their unfulfilled ambitions as human beings. They asked themselves whether they were case-hardened; and what effect their work had on their personal life and relationships. Each took it in turn to play the role of one of his own subordinates, giving himself honest feedback on what it was really like to work under him. And so on.

After several hours of this they staggered out into the September sunshine spaced out of their minds. At the end of the five days, after their time with the sociology people and the computing unit, they had a review of the whole course. I was unable to attend this, but I was told they went on and on about the educational impact of the first two days. They even sent a deputation to the Vice-Chancellor's office to ask why they had never heard of that kind of education before. Then I realised that here was an opening. Looking at established institutions in terms of a hierarchy of social control, the police outrank universities: if students are revolting, it is the police who wade in with tear gas and batons, while academic staff are sequestered nervously in their studies. If a radical method is commended by the police, a university must take notice. I said to David James: "If it is possible to have such a response with senior police offers, this is surely a mandate to offer this educational method to other professional groups and the general public". And so the Human Potential Research Project was born. As I said, rigid systems are porous: there are always openings, spaces between the lines of the grid in which you can plant flowers.

# 17  Personhood and spiritual inquiry

## Theological personalism

The guiding ideas behind my practice of spiritual inquiry can be set forth in seven basic statements. They constitute a version of theological personalism in the European tradition of mystical philosophers like Martin Buber (1937) and Nikolai Berdyaev (1937), updated in terms of a participatory worldview (Abram, 1996; Bateson, 1979; Ferrer, 2002; Heron, 1992, 1996a, 1998; Heron and Reason, 1997; Merleau-Ponty, 1962; Reason, 1994; Skolimowski, 1994; Spretnak, 1991; Tarnas, 1991), a series of co-operative inquiries, and my personal lived inquiry into Being (Heron, 1998). Here are the statements. A human person:

- Is a distinct spiritual presence in, and nonseparable from, the given cosmos, participating through immediate present experience - the very process of being in a world - in the presence of the divine.

- Is not to be reduced to, or confused with, an illusory, separate, contracted, and egoic self with which personhood can become temporarily identified.

- Emerges from and is grounded in immanent spiritual life; and is informed and illuminated by a transcendent spiritual consciousness.

- Has original revelation here and now, through opening to his or her intrinsic saturation with divinity. Such revelation is a human-divine communion, a co-creation of mediated-immediacy.

- Has spiritual authority within which, when freed from the distortions of spiritual projection onto external sources, manifests as co-created inner light and inner life.

- Has freedom to generate, with immanent spiritual life, an innovative spiritual path.

- Manifests the creative process of divine becoming as an autonomous being, embedded in connectedness, and in co-operative, transformative relations with other persons similarly engaged.

In an earlier book, *Feeling and Personhood* (Heron, 1992), I suggested that there are various states of personhood, which I called primal, spontaneous, compulsive, conventional, creative, self-creating, self-transfiguring, and charismatic; and looked at various possible relations between them, and possible patterns of personal development in which they figure. The self-transfiguring person I portrayed as one who:

> ...has embarked upon the realization of their subtle energies, psychic capacities and spiritual potentials. They are busy with transformations of ordinary perception and action, extra sensory development and access to other realities, ritual, meditation, prayer, worship, and living in the now. And all this is integrated with a creative, expressive life in the world. (Heron, 1992: 61)

The present essay focuses on the self-transfiguring person adopting a path of lived inquiry. I will discuss the above seven statements in more detail, refining and advancing the views put forward in *Sacred Science* (Heron, 1998).

## The participatory person

*1. A person is a distinct spiritual presence in, and nonseparable from, the given cosmos, participating through immediate present experience - the very process of being in a world - in the presence of the divine.*

*2. As such, a person is not to be reduced to, or confused with, an illusory, separate, contracted and egoic self with which personhood can become temporarily identified.*

I find that my everyday self is always and inalienably immersed in divinity simply by virtue of its way of being in a world. The process of my perceiving - visual, auditory, tactile, kinesthetic imaging - is relational, interactive, interdependent and correlative. There is no gap, no separation between I the imager, the imaging, and the imaged. This unitive process enacts a local world with infinite, unlimited horizons without, and emerges from a generative infinitude within. The enactment is tacitly continuous with these dipolar infinities. I am engaged with cosmic imagination: "The living power and prime agent of all human perception and a repetition in the finite mind of the eternal act of creation in the infinite I AM" (Coleridge).

Moreover, my perceiving is not only imaging, it is at the same time a felt mutual resonance with what is being imaged. This tells us that we, the entities present, in the totality of our reciprocal relations, constitute the sheer vibrant presence of Being here and now. I call this, simply, immediate present experience. This is already a religious experience: the communion of self and world within the embrace of Being.

Without this going on all the time, there is no world for the everyday self. At the same time my self can get dissociated and distracted from its necessary participatory nature. It can get constricted in the illusory separateness of an alienated ego structure: by childhood wounding; by the exigencies of survival and social life; by the way the concepts that come with language separate subject from object, imager from imaged, bury the participatory transaction of imaging, and distract attention from felt resonance (Heron, 1992).

However, by paying attention to these three factors, and by learning how to disperse their constricting impact, I can uncover what has been going on all the time - interactive imaging and resonance within the presence of Being here and now. This uncovering and coming to my senses reveals a real person in relation with other centres of reference. As such:

- I am unique by having a standpoint and viewpoint, an enactive perspective. Whereas the self as contracted ego has to do with illusory separateness, the self as emergent person has to do with a distinct perspective within real unity.

- I am constituted by mutual engagement with others in a world, participating reciprocally in the presence of other beings, human and non-human, within the presence of Being.

- I image their forms of appearing, make discriminatory judgments about their status and significance, and choose to act in relation to them.

- I am capable of extensive and intensive unfoldment by virtue of an inherent opening onto an infinite actuality without and beyond, and an infinite potential within. I can creatively transform my world, and be a catalyst to transfigure myself.

This immediate present experience, this being one of the here and now Many-in-relation-in-the-One, is the locus and foundation of personhood. It is not prepersonal, not prior to verbal and conceptual mastery. I have called it post-linguistic and post-conceptual (Heron, 1992, 1996a), to mean simply that it follows from deconstructing the subject-object split that language-use imposes on the process of perceiving. It is a person participating intentionally in local, temporal divine presence, and poised at the interface between transcendent spiritual consciousness and immanent spiritual life. From this here and now, the ongoing spiritual process is one of rhythmic expansion, increasing the present wholeness through a spiraling inclusion of hitherto immanent and transcendent spirit, with various intermittent phases of consolidation and reactive contraction.

A person on my view, then, is an embodied spiritual presence, one of the real Many within the divine One, whose distinctness of being within the unity of the whole is more fundamental than any of her or his temporary and illusory states of egoic alienation and separateness. This distinctness of a person has to do with him or her being one unique focus, among many, of the whole web of interbeing relations. Personal autonomy is grounded in this unique presence, participating resonantly in an unitive field of interconnected beings, within the presence of Being. It is manifest as the individual perspective necessarily involved in imaging a world, as the individual judgment inalienably required to make relevant distinctions and evaluations according to appropriate standards, and as individual responsibility in choosing to act.

This is not the personal autonomy of the Cartesian ego, an isolated, self-reflexive consciousness independent of any context - what Charlene Spretnak calls the Lone Cowboy sense of autonomy. It is, rather,

> The ecological/cosmological sense of uniqueness coupled with intersubjectivity and interbeing...One can accurately speak of the 'autonomy' of an individual only by incorporating a sense of the dynamic web of relationships that are constitutive for that being at a given moment (Spretnak, 1995: 5).

This web or context has two layers. There is the superficial linguistic, cultural context within which autonomy is exercised and by which it is socially defined. And there is the deeper primary, extralinguistic and extracultural, context of *conscious* mutual participation with other presences in given Being, within which autonomy can also be intentionally exercised and by which it is, so to say, divinely defined.

### The person and dipolar divine dynamics

*3. A person emerges from and is grounded in immanent spiritual life; and is informed and illuminated by a transcendent spiritual consciousness.*

I hold a provisional theory of the divine as encompassing:

- Transcendent spiritual consciousness, beyond and informing our immediate experience.

- Immanent spiritual life, deep within and animating our immediate experience. And, mediating between the poles

- Our very present immediate experience of here and now form and process.

I also find that it makes sense of my experience of the inner heights and depths, to integrate this dipolarity of transcendent consciousness and immanent life, with another mysterious one, the dipolarity of the manifest and the unmanifest. The term 'unmanifest' is not very satisfactory, does not reside in the dictionary, so I shall replace with both 'beyond-the-manifest' and 'within-the-manifest'.

Thus I encounter transcendent consciousness as *beyond-the-manifest*: as boundless ineffability, ecstatic infinitude beyond all form and differentiation, beyond every circumference, every defining name. I also find that transcendent consciousness is *manifest* in two complementary ways. It is as if it generates all spatial form in some sense and also upholds it. So I engage with it as originating sound and light, creative overmind, demiurge, the first word of form. And then, too, I meet it as all-holding universal mind, cosmic store-consciousness, the repository of informing archetypes.

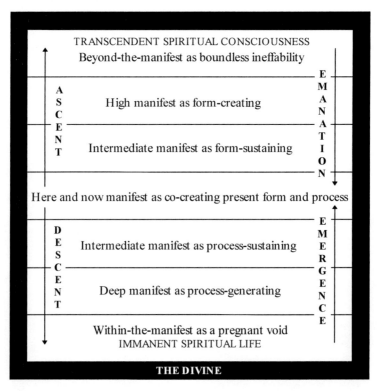

*Figure 7: Dipolar theology and the dipolar spiritual path*

Plumbing the depths of immanent life I engage with the mystery of the within-the-manifest: primordial emptiness, the infinitude within all form, within every centre the essential absence within all differentiation, the spaceless womb of being. At the same pole, immanent life manifests in complementary ways, both generating temporal process and sustaining it. So I feel it as generative, primordial life, the living emergence of new development from within, the inner, innovative prompt to time my own process in this or that or the other way. And I also feel it as interfused and pervasive inner presence, manifest as the sustaining cyclic gestures in time, both of the presence that I am in the world, and of the diverse presences of the world with whom I am in mutual exchange.

The integrative centre between the poles is my immediate present experience of being now here, my consciousness-life co-creating present form and process in conjunction with divine consciousness-life. I participate in a unitive field of being-in-a-world: present in an immediate, local, participatory subjective-objective reality, in which there is no gap between subject and object, between perceiver, perceiving and perceived, between consciousness and its contents, between resonant feeling and other diverse presences, between form and process, between my being and my becoming. This explicit local unitive field is full of distinctions and motions without separateness. It is partial, capable of expansion and contraction, and is the explicit innovative focus of active becoming within a tacit ground of infinite height, depth and extent.

Figure 7 above sets out in diagrammatic form this dipolar theology, the arrows on the right portraying dipolar divine dynamics, and the arrows on the left suggesting a dipolar spiritual path. For the divine dynamics read from the bottom to the middle and from the top to the middle. For the spiritual path, read from the middle to the bottom and from the middle to the top. Remember, it is just a construct, a modest metaphor, a simplifying device. But it does, so far as it can, resonate beyond itself to that which is true to my experience. It has been elaborated in the cartography presented in *Sacred Science* (Heron, 1998).

**The person and original revelation**

*4. A person has original revelation here and now through opening to his or her intrinsic saturation with divinity. Such revelation is a human-divine communion, a co-creation of mediated-immediacy.*

I regard spiritual inquiry as a process of co-creative communion with the divine, involving human mediation of the immediacy of divine presence. By the divine, as we have seen, I mean that astonishing presence that transcends, includes and is immanent within, all manifest realms, both subtle and material.

The belief that the divine is a One-Many reality that includes everything, means that the process of spiritual inquiry is itself a form of divine becoming. It is part of god exploring its relation with the rest of god and the whole of god. The human inquirer is one of the divine Many entering into discriminating communion with the rest of the Many and the One. And as one of the Many, the human inquirer is intrinsically saturated with divinity.

The notion of intrinsic saturation points to what is already the case about our being in the world, but from which we can readily be distracted from noticing. So a basic kind of inquiry is the practice of opening to this that is already the case. What I call 'intrinsic saturation' is similar to what Karl Rahner calls 'transcendental experience', a universal pre-reflective and tacit experience of god which is the foundation for all other human experience, and which becomes conscious only when we reflect deeply on the conditions for the possibility of human knowledge and activity (Kelly, 1993). Merleau-Ponty, coming in from a different angle, also spoke of 'radical reflection' which reveals the fusion of seer and seen in and through the 'flesh', a fusion which is prior to and a condition of all subsequent analysis (Bernasconi, 1995).

Intrinsic saturation - what is already the case - is revealed by reflective contemplation, a process of self-transcending reflection which both encounters the divinity it formulates, and is formulated by that divinity, in a co-creative embrace. Contemplation of the mutual encounter, dwelling in the communion of one of the Many and the One, transcends the purely reflective process by which it is entered. What starts out as mental mediation becomes mediated-immediacy, a co-creative human-divine communion. What is divine in it has universal validity, the human mediation in it makes it relative to the context of its formulation. The notion of mediated-immediacy stands on the middle ground between the extremes of contextualist relativism and absolutist universalism (for a related view see Ferrer, 2002).

Kant used a form of transcendental argument to provide a priori knowledge of the world as it appears, but not as it is in itself. His epistemology is self-enclosing: it cuts us off from radical ontology, from being-as-such. Self-transcending reflection is rather different: it yields a priori knowledge which mediates the immediacy of what there is, encountered in and through the epiphany of its appearing. Epistemology and ontology merge in a co-shaping communion of knowing and being (cf. Panikkar, 1996).

Here are some examples of intrinsic saturation which can become conscious through reflective contemplation of the kind I have described; and which I invite the reader to check out in his or her own lived inquiry. I present them mainly in terms of a brief phenomenology of their contemplative states. For a fuller account of the prior reflections see Heron (1992, Chapters 5, 7, 8, 9; 1996a, Chapter 10; 1998, Parts 1 and 3). And note that the fourth of the examples below, on intention, goes beyond self-transcending reflection into the realm of self-transcending practical knowing, self-transfiguring knowing-how.

*4.1. Perception.* Human perceiving is grounded in human feeling, which I differentiate from emotion, and regard as the capacity of a person to participate as a distinct non-separate presence in wider unities of being (Heron, 1992). In such radical perception, there is no gap, no separation between perceiver and perceived. Subject and object, which may also be another human subject, interfuse in a co-creative embrace. This consciousness-world, or person-to-person, co-participatory union is the local home of the go-between divinity, the living presence of *Shekinah* (in Jewish tradition a feminine word for divine immanence), the manifest goddess alive in the reality of relationship. Furthermore, both centre and circumference of finite perceiving - the sensory world-field of *Shekinah* - are fraught with an inalienable engagement with the infinite.

If you attend to the centre of reference for touch, kinesthetic sense, seeing and hearing, it is a delicious void, there is nothing there. It is an infinitude within. These four modalities of imaging our being-in-a-world coalesce at an apparent locus which they declare to be a full emptiness. It is full because it is a cornucopia out of which our whole four-modal world pours. And it is empty because it is a womb of internal infinitude.

Likewise every perceptual circumference or boundary, every finite limit to the seeing and hearing of our sensory field, declares its latent infinity. Each limit declares there is more beyond it. It announces a series of limits that is unlimited. In one horizon we have tacit acquaintance with horizons that are infinite. But the infinite is not the finite horizon that is never met, it is the transcendent ground and condition of the whole series, implicit in each and every horizon. Explicit participation in any one of the bounded is a tacit participation in the transcendent boundless, *das Umgreifende*. The unlimited, the infinite, the boundless transcends the series of contexts it defines. Through the circumscription of our perceiving we engage with the ineffable, the ecstatic, the standing outside of any determinate setting or series of such settings, which yet contains them all.

So here in our very being-in-the-world of perceiving we are saturated with the tri-partite face of god: the manifest presence alive in the reality of relationship, the immanent generative void at our centre of reference, and the transcendent ineffable boundless crowning every horizon.

*4.2. Motivation.* Human motivation with all its everyday finite limits of desire and want and need is rooted in an infinite potential. Needs are the manifest of our capacities, most basically for loving and knowing and choosing. There are all sorts of ongoing, contingent limits - culminating in this world in physical death - to our expression of these capacities. But it makes no sense to talk of a limit to the fulfilment of these capacities that is intrinsic to their nature. Just to say that this or that is the inherent limit of our loving or our knowing or our choosing, is to become tacitly engaged with what lies beyond the supposed limit. Every determinate stage of the development of our human capacities is sooner or later riven with a self-transcending yearning, a hunger for the tacit whole of Being.

On the holonomic principle, just as the genetic potential of the whole human body is present in each of its cells, so the whole of the One-Many is present in each inquiring one of the Many as his or her infinite potential. This is Schelling's *deus implicitus,* spirit-in-action, the divine self-transcending drive at the root of human motivation: the drive of each one to open to the heights and depths of the One and manifest an ever more distinctive lustre within the collegiality of the Many. We long to be open to the One. We long for collegiality - unbound mutuality and co-inherence of distinctness of being without separation of being, individual diversity in free unity.

Theologians, East and West, have had a range of delicious terms for co-inherence - *circuminsessio, conciliarité, koinonia, perichoresis, sobornost* - and these now call for general release beyond the reach of church dogmatics. Following Solovyov in the nineteenth century, Berdyaev (1937) in the twentieth century gives the best generalized account of the best of these terms - *sobornost* - as the creative process of divine spirit manifest through the self-determining subjectivity of human personhood, engaged in the realization of value and achieved in true community.

*4.3. Attention.* Human attention is at the core of everyday awareness: we attend to this and we attend to that. It is the very focus of our effective in-the-world consciousness. Yet when we attend to this attentive capacity, when we rest our focus on this focus, on itself, it becomes a lens which refracts a vast expanse of transpersonal awareness, a soaring outreach of universal intelligence of which our own attention to daily life is the local manifest. Such vigilant awareness of its own stillness opens to the cosmic ocean of consciousness.

Another version of this route is via transcendental subjectivity, in Kant's jargon 'the transcendental unity of apperception', the a priori unity of consciousness on which all coherence and meaning of inner and outer experience depend. The 'I' transcends any account it gives of itself, since it is the ever-present pre-condition of every account. To attend to the 'I', to be in the 'I', both in and beyond any determinate description of itself, is to open to its consubstantiality with the great 'I', that consciousness that embraces whatever there is. This is one-One consubstantiality: since the 'I' can always give an appropriate developing account of itself, it is a distinct one of the Many; since it always absolutely transcends this account, it is contained in the One.

*4.4. Intention.* The notion of intention is a crucial ingredient in an account of human action and agency. Act-related intentions, that is, intentions involved in particular present behaviours, are the hall-mark of the human agent. Such intentions are a compound of (1) the purpose of the action, its end, aim or intended outcome; (2) its means, strategy or method of achieving that purpose; and (3) the actual physical behaviours - the movements, postures, gestures, breath and sounds - required to implement the means. Human agents are much preoccupied with the ends and means of actions as determined by the prevailing beliefs, norms and values of the social system of which they are a daily part. The bodily processes involved are subservient to this pre-occupation.

But suppose now the physical behaviours - the movements, postures, gestures, breath and sounds - become both the end and the means. The purpose of the action is to manifest their intrinsic dynamism, which is also the method of fulfilling that purpose. Both purpose and method are for action to speak out in its own extralinguistic mode. Action then becomes self-transcending sacred posture, movement and sound, creating a spatio-temporal matrix of divine presence. This matrix is a holonomic celebration of, and a performative participation in, the divine Act generating spatio-temporal worlds galore. The body reveals itself as a dynamic ambassador of cosmic grace.

Inquirers here are being intentional about going deeper into their embodiment to manifest the indwelling life divine, as it moves through the total fabric of creation, physical and subtle. They co-create spatio-temporal matrices with this emerging dynamic divine potential not only through impromptu sacred posture, movement and sound, but also rhythmic breathing and body work, rhythmic emotional cleansing and healing. The everyday ends and means of social life can be interfused with further matrices through charismatic bearing and gesture, charismatic timing and tone of voice. And through intentional human-divine co-creation of the rhythms of living and loving: waking and sleeping, activity and relaxation, eating and fasting, sexuality and celibacy, creativity and lying fallow, coming and going, togetherness and separation, communality and privacy, autonomy and co-operation, caring and confrontation, innovation and conservation; and of the physical, energetic and psychic rhythms of the day, the week, the month, the year and its seasons, and longer cycles.

*4.5. Judgment.* A human being is pre-eminently a judging being. To become a person is to learn how to differentiate and discriminate, to make relevant distinctions, and to evaluate in various ways what has thus been distinguished. The ability to judge - to differentiate and evaluate according to appropriate standards - needs education, training, practice; but it is necessarily self-directed, no-one else can do it for us. Once acquired, it makes us autonomous adults, capable of entering into genuine co-operation and collegiality, authentic diversity in unity. Distinguish in order to unite, said Maritain.

The autonomous 'I' who makes the judgment, a distinct person among the Many, is contingently this and that sort of person, but is ultimately and necessarily not this, not that. It is the transcendental subject who is the author of all the differentiations made, including self-differentiations, while at the same time being their undifferentiated ground. This is one-One autonomy, personal autonomy intrinsically immersed in divine unity and in the collegiality of the Many. Personal autonomy is itself at root human-divine, mediated-immediacy.

The most radical judgments any human can make are about the divine and a relationship with the divine. It follows from the above, that if these judgments are not autonomous, they are not divinely grounded. They are heteronomous, dependent on, and co-determined with, teacher, tradition or text. They are pseudo-divine. Of course, it may be our autonomous judgment that a teacher, tradition or text offers us a way forward for a while. But only for a while, otherwise we rapidly relapse into heteronomy and the cul-de-sac of other-directed salvation.

## The person and internal authority

*5. A person has spiritual authority within which, when freed from the distortions of spiritual projection onto external sources, manifests as co-created inner light and inner life.*

If we claim that spiritual authority resides in some other person, being, doctrine, book, school or church, we are the legitimating author of this claim. We choose to regard it as valid. No authority resides in anything external unless we first decide to confer that authority on it. Nothing out there is accredited and definitive until we first elect it to be so. All explicit judgments that illumination resides without, rest upon a prior and much more basic tacit light within. When it is made explicit, this is the internal authority of which our own discriminating judgment is the expression. Individual human judgment, with its inner spiritual ground, is the legitimating source of all external spiritual authority. The religious history of the human race appears to involve the slow and painful realization that this is indeed the case.

> We have to realize that every revelation must finally be appropriated by the individual soul. The very term 'revelation' implies the existence of the minds by which it is received. And it is on the attitude of such minds that everything in the end depends. The last word is with the interior monitor. The process is not completed until the divine which appears without is acknowledged by the divine which is enthroned deep within. And no amount of ingenious sophistry can do away with this ultimate fact. In other words the individual must take his stand upon the witness of the inner light, the authority within his own soul. This principle was clearly formulated by the Cambridge Platonist, Benjamin Whichcote, who ventured on the statement: 'If you have a revelation from God, I must have a revelation from God too before I can believe you'. (Hyde, 1949: 39)

When we become aware that the final court of spiritual authority resides within, and that any authority we had vested in anyone or anything external was derived from the imprimatur of that inner court, then we are spiritually centreed and will not in the future become improperly subservient to any religious school. What we learn from it will be passed through the prism of our inner discrimination. But when we are not aware of this, then we are busy with spiritual projection, and are spiritually off-centre. The spiritual authority that resides within is not known for what it is, is in some sense suppressed and denied, and is then unconsciously projected on, invested in, *and inevitably misrepresented and distorted by,* what is without.

If our internal authorizing of a spiritual teacher is displaced and projected out as an external authority residing in that teacher, then our inner authority is misrepresented as nescience seeking illumination from another, instead of being affirmed as our inner knowing seeking dialogue with the inner knowing of another. Thus we deny the divine ground of our own autonomous judgment, and become followers, second-class spiritual citizens in a heteronomous culture, inescapably excluded from authentic enlightenment.

When we are fully aware of spiritual projection so that it can be substantially withdrawn and undone, then the spiritual path itself is based on internal authority through the continuous exercise of our own discriminating judgment and its spiritual ground; and this in association with others similarly engaged. Divine becoming emerges as the living spiritual ground of human autonomy and co-operation. And the divinity thus manifest will necessarily be different in certain fundamental respects, in terms of beliefs and practices, from all divinities defined by external authorities. However, there are three very important caveats about all this, the second being the crucial one.

First, such withdrawal is not an all or nothing phenomenon. It may involve a variety of hybrids. These include:

- *Sequential projection.* A person projects for a period on one spiritual school, then withdraws it and projects on to another, going through several over a number of years. This process may become quite intentional, in the sense that the person consciously goes along with the authoritarian tendency of a school in order to benefit from its teachings and practices, and pulls out when that tendency becomes too spiritually restricting.

- *Partial projection.* A person stays constantly within one tradition in allegiance to certain strands of it, while radically reappraising other strands.

- *Intellectual freedom.* The intellect appears to exercise a lot of freedom, for example, with respect to transpersonal theory, but practice remains firmly wedded to projection within a spiritual school. The theoretical outcome will then include veiled special pleading for the practical allegiance.

- *Discreet freedom.* A person remains within one tradition for purposes of the support found within its spiritual community, otherwise picks and chooses among its beliefs and practices, refracting them through the prism of the internal monitor.

Second, and crucially, I doubt whether there is a final end to the process of spiritual projection. There is certainly a critical point when it is raised into consciousness and radically withdrawn as human-divine autonomy is reclaimed. But this reclamation, this radical reappraisal of one's spirituality, may well include elements drawn from past and present spiritual practitioners and thinkers. So the reappraisal, in weeding out past projections, may rely, in part and on occasion, on new ones in order to do so. The difference, of course, is in the awareness that this may be going on. Hence the critical subjectivity of a reframing mind, which continually deconstructs presumed internal authority to uncover any projections that may be at work displacing it. The authority within, being co-created, mediated-immediacy, is never final, always provisional. Its divine immediacy makes it a revelation, its human mediation makes it a fallible one. This is one of the deepest practical paradoxes of the religious life.

Thirdly, the substantial withdrawal of spiritual projection from traditional and new age schools certainly does not mean that one ceases to take account of them and learn anything from them. On the contrary, the beliefs and practices of the various schools, ancient and modern, constitute a huge data-bank, a massive resource which, when refracted through the internal monitor, can be drawn upon, adapted and revised in framing the maps which guide autonomous and co-operative spiritual inquiry.

In the opening statement to this section, I define spiritual authority simply as inner light and inner life. Before elaborating this, let's be clear that I cannot be an external authority defining the nature of internal authority for others. Self-direction cannot be other-defined and other-prescribed. Autonomous people can only dialogue and inquire with each other about the nature of self-direction. Here, then, are some of my conjectures on the matter, based on my own lived inquiry, and put forward as a contribution to such dialogue .

By 'inner light' I mean the discriminating judgment of the distinct person and its transcendent source, the one-to-One, which I have described above. By 'inner life' I mean impulses from the divine ground of human motivation, mentioned above. Inner light is the critical subjectivity by which intelligent judgments are made about things spiritual. Inner life is the impulse to open to Being, to make self-transfiguring and self-transcending choices.

This dipolarity of spiritual life and light is the great pincer movement of awakening: on the one hand the inner impulse to open to Being, on the other hand the discriminating realization that we are already saturated with it.

To say some more about inner life, I find that my everyday psyche has a very evident supporting ground or foundation. When I attend to this ground, it becomes a source or well-spring, which, when I open to it, is of apparently limitless potential. It is also like a cornucopia or womb, with an ever-deepening infinitude within. Its potential fullness increases as I plumb its depth and creative darkness, and so does its emptiness.

I call this spiritual life within, since it is harbors spiritseed, entelechy, the formative potential of my becoming. The spiritseed puts out sprouts, shoots - above ground in the psyche. They are prompts to open to Being, and to time or space my being, in relation to the immediate context of interbeing, in this, that or the other way. Inner light, my discriminating awakening to a wider consciousness, is in dialogic relation with these inner life-prompts.

This internal dialogue between inner light and inner life is, further, in interaction with what I regard as a third contributor to inner spiritual authority - appropriate discourse with the other, upon which I elaborate under statement 7 below.

**The person and spiritual innovation**

*6. A person has freedom to generate, with immanent spiritual life, an innovative spiritual path.*

I said just above that the spiritual life within harbors spiritseed, entelechy, the formative potential of my becoming. What Aristotle meant by an entelechy was the condition in which a potentiality has become an actuality. But there is another more recent usage in which entelechy is the immanent, formative potential of what is actual. So the entelechy guides the emergence of, and is progressively realized in, the actual entity.

Carl Rogers made this idea of entelechy a basic tenet of his personality theory. He called it an actualizing tendency. He thought it was inborn in everyone as an "inherent tendency of the organism to develop all its capacities in ways which serve to maintain or enhance the organism" (Rogers, 1959: 196). "It is clear that the actualizing tendency is selective and directional - a constructive tendency" (Rogers, 1980: 121).

It affects both body and mind, and with respect to the latter, it guides people toward increased autonomy, expanded experience and inner growth. Virtually the same idea is found in Maslow, as a self-actualizing need, "the desire to become more and more what one idiosyncratically is, to become everything one is capable of becoming" (Maslow, 1970: 46).

It reappears in Wilber as the Ground-Unconscious which is "all the deep structures existing as potentials ready to emerge at some future point" (Wilber, 1990: 105). And in Washburn as the "Dynamic Ground (libido, psychic energy, numinous power or spirit) of somatic, instinctual, affective and creative-imaginal potentials" (Washburn, 1995: 11). Jean Houston writes of the Entelechy Self as "the Root Self, the ground of one's being, and the seeded coded essence in you which contains both the patterns and the possibilities of your life". (Houston, 1987:31). These three writers all use the metaphor of the ground in characterizing the spiritual life-potential within.

Do these ground potentials act upon us willy-nilly, predetermining the basic stages of our explicit spiritual development? Do they constitute a fixed pattern of our future unfolding? Alternatively, do the ground potentials offer a range of possibilities from among which we may choose and so create our own pattern? I take this second view. I believe that we may co-create our path in dynamic relation with a set of options emerging from the spiritual life within. And this not only in relation to the daily surface structure of the path, but also concerning its basic unfolding pattern. *Radical spiritual innovation is the hallmark of divine becoming.*

Of course, we must at any given time entertain a working hypothesis of some basic array of options for developing our divine potential, if we are effectively to set about actualizing it. But what this array is, what general constants it contains, and by what sequence it may be realized over time, are for each of us undetermined matters until we start on our own path. They are open to co-creation with immanent spirit, through processes of individual and co-operative inquiry, and taking account of prior inquiries and the legacy of diverse spiritual traditions.

There is great scope for future spiritual innovation here. Indeed, when autonomous people relate within an ongoing self-generating spiritual culture, and the path for each becomes significantly interactive, the potential for emergent novelty in path-making is hugely increased. This does not make for a chaotic, anything-goes, relativism, but for unity in real diversity. The universal divine constants are necessarily revealed in and through the variations of human-divine innovation.

Can one enter into a conscious co-creating relation with immanent spiritual life, its womb of possibility? I believe so. You can relate to it, give it voice and be spiritually upheld and nourished by it, and enter into a co-guiding dynamic with it. I say co-guiding, since you select and shape the guiding as much as the guiding shapes you. This, on the one hand, makes it maculate, corrigible, and personally autonomous, and on the other hand reveals divine immediacy.

Various techniques have been proposed, in recent times, for tapping directly into the guiding potential within. E-Therapy was one (Kitselman, 1953). Kitselman asks how we can let out the greatness that is in us and affirms that it can let itself out, it only needs to be asked. He then outlines a simple technique for asking E, the inner voice, which will respond in terms of any one or more of the following: inner ecstatic fire, trembling, body movements, disidentification from personal history, or an impulse toward some strategic action.

The much researched experiential focusing of Gendlin is another (Gendlin, 1981). This basically consists in making a clear relaxed area in the body-mind so that when a key question - suitably refined and focused - is asked, there is space for the answer to be manifest, in verbal or nonverbal imagery, accompanied by a subtle release of energy. Gendlin describes the whole process as if it were primarily somatic, a description which has always seemed to me to be rather too cautious.

But McMahon and Campbell develop Gendlin's focusing in terms of a bio-spiritual approach. Their bio-spirituality emphasizes "an experience of grace in the body". They relate letting go into the body-feeling about an issue, to a movement of the indwelling life-giving presence and power of God (McMahon and Campbell, 1991: 5, 17).

None of these processes is a purely passive receptivity to some guiding internal otherness, although they have a tendency to be described in this way, as I have just done in order to report them in their own terms. But my experience of them, and of related sorts of inner lived inquiry, is that my subjectivity is actively involved at a deep level in selecting and shaping life-processes moving within. The challenge of these methods is not to surrender fully to what comes up from the depths, but to open up that liberated place within where one can be co-creative with immanent spirit. And this with respect to options that shape both the surface and deeper pattern of the spiritual path.

**The person and transformative connectedness**

*7. A person manifests the creative process of divine becoming as an autonomous being, embedded in connectedness, and in co-operative, transformative relations with other persons similarly engaged.*

In terms of process theology (Hartshorne and Reese, 1953), one aspect of divinity is the temporal becoming of finite entities within an infinite field. This includes self-determining human subjectivity, whose inner light and life, in interaction as I have described above, is in process of development, in the context of the limited flux and turn of events accessible to the individual. Both the inner light and the inner life are human-divine co-creations, forms of mediated-immediacy, hence they are maculate, corrigible, relative to their setting, changing and unfolding. At the human end, they are subject to three limiting factors.

- My social context, the hermeneutic situation of local language and culture.

- The degree of my explicit, conscious participation in the interbeing of the universe, the collective field of reciprocally engaged and diverse presences.

- The degree of emotional damage and spiritual constriction within which I labor.

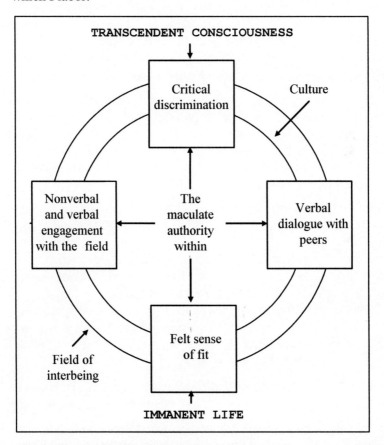

*Figure 8: The maculate authority within*

Hence the importance of both critical subjectivity and life-prompts being exercised within a community of peers, who assist each other - using a range of peer support procedures - with the rigor of continuous spiritual deconstruction. Such deconstruction means being aware of how these three factors interact and how the presuppositions of this interaction set the scene for, limit and mould, every act of inner light and inner life. It means an attitude of bracketing such presuppositions and being open to their reframing through, respectively, a revision of prevailing belief-systems in the culture, enriched participation in the lived-through world, and emotional healing. Persons in peer groups can do a variety of things together to facilitate these three undertakings.

Such deconstruction does not eliminate or dethrone either the inner light or the inner life. On the contrary, it empowers each to flourish with ever greater temporary relevance. This maculate authority within is shown in Figure 8. The word 'maculate' is the opposite of 'immaculate', which means free from fault, perfect, spotless. So 'maculate' means not free from fault, imperfect, spotted. I also take it to mean relative to its limited context, and good enough in relation to its context. Thus the 'macula lutea' is the region of greatest visual acuity in the retina of the eye.

So as well as exercising discriminating inner light, and opening to the impulses of spiritual life, there is an important third contributor to the spiritual authority within. It is appropriate discourse with the other. This brings the internal dialogue between inner light and inner life into a comprehensive and more-than-verbal, as well as a verbal, relation with others in their world.

Everything is talking to everything else in the primordial language of creation. Abram eloquently makes the point in his *The Spell of the Sensuous,* that we do not inhabit a purely external, objective world out there, but a world of *intersubjective* phenomena in which human and non-human presences of all kinds forma shared field of experience lived through from diverse viewpoints. Within this participatory field, with which we reciprocally engage, there is an animate process of mutual apprehension - a meaningful dialogue of interbeing - going on. And this is prior to, and the ground and source of, all our use of verbal language (Abram, 1996; Heron, 1996a).

So my phrase 'appropriate discourse with the other' is inclusive. It means several things:

- Opening now to nonverbal, interbeing exchange with the presences that are here, which we name trees and roads, rocks and stars, fish and fowl; and with the sheer presence of the whole in all its modes, physical, subtle and spiritual. This, I find, is a primal revelation of the divine. It is the dynamic eminence of the immediate multidimensional experiential world, the here and now collective field, in which our own presence is in reciprocal engagement, through being and doing, with other diverse presences, within the presence of Being. This nonverbal exchange may, for the person involved, be a silent, still and enriched participation in terms of felt resonance and imaging. Or it may be nonverbally expressive, embodying this participatory engagement in vocal or musical sounds, movements, gestures and postures; or in impromptu drawing, painting and modeling of clay.

- Talking to, talking with, talking within, this field - out loud and out of doors in my native tongue - using a variety of metaphors and figures of speech. In this process I am hearing what I am moved to say, how I am moved to edit and reframe it - and so deepen my encounter with Being - as I engage with the collective field of experience in which I am embodied and embedded. I am attending to a subtle dialogue between verbal and nonverbal forms of utterance and participation.

- The above practices - the silent and still, the nonverbally expressive, and the verbally improvised - can be variously combined in a charismatic collaborative inquiry into Being, by a group of spiritual inquirers, working sometimes simultaneously, and sometimes serially. This becomes a celebratory, innovative inquiry at the immediate, dynamic crest of divine becoming. For more details see the account of 'primary theatre' in Heron (2001b, Chapter 8; 1999, Chapters 11 and 12).

- Dialogue with other humans, sharing our intelligent judgments and views, apprehensions and intuitions, about things spiritual and subtle. It can have two forms, verbal and aesthetic. We can talk with words, or we can exchange aesthetic presentations, nonverbal symbols of our spiritual process, wrought in any one or more of the whole range of art-forms. There is thus possible a mutual fructification between the propositional and the presentational, between explanation and expression (Heron, 1996a: 88-90).

The view of internal spiritual authority which I have presented can be construed, in Berdyaev's terms, as the creative, temporal process of divine becoming, which manifests as human-divine autonomy, a dipolar inner light and inner life, and evaluates that creative process in collaboration with other presences and persons in the field of interbeing. This means cultivation of discriminatory competence in evaluating spiritual and subtle events, of openness to impulses from the spiritual life deep within, of relationship with the felt field of interbeing, and reviewing the whole process in dialogue with one's peers.

My basic postulate about the field of interbeing, is that any presence within it is uniquely what it is interdependently with the particular structure of the web of relations within which it is a nodal point or focus. No entity is distinct apart from its interconnections with other entities. Individual agency is correlative with social communion. Just so, human persons are only persons in relation with other persons. I can only be genuinely autonomous when in authentic co-operation with others.

Seeing the world as temporal divine process, I find true religion among autonomous humans in co-operative relations with each other and with the more-than-human world, taking account also of presences in complementary realities. I enter into union between beings, and with Being as such, when each being is both individualized and participatory. As we transcend separateness and alienation we become both more distinct and more in communion with each other. Our becoming more refined, autonomous and discriminating in our judgments, is interdependent with our entering ever more fully into participatory relations and unitive embrace. This is *sobornost,* One-Many sacrality, crowned by the transcendent and grounded in the immanent.

At present, co-operative inquiry (Heron and Reason, 2001; Heron 1996a; Reason, 1988, 1994) in the spiritual sphere is unused and unknown, and is threatening to the authoritarianism that is part and parcel both of a long-standing spiritual traditions and of brash new spiritual cults. Such research means that a group of spiritual inquirers explore mystical and subtle experience together and discriminate among themselves about it (Heron, 2001a, 1998). They can:

- Devise practices consonant with their inner light and life, and thus give form to their own original relation to creation.

- Elicit categories of understanding appropriate to their experience, without relapsing unconsciously into traditional doctrines, new age euphoria, or culturally prevalent beliefs and values.

- Refine the authority within - the discriminating inner light, the grounding inner life and the deconstruction of any ongoing projection - by the collaborative use of inquiry cycles and validity procedures.

- Clarify practical issues about entering and exiting from the experience.

- Winnow out criteria for distinguishing spiritual experience from purely psychological or subtle states.

- Manifest, as central to the inquiry process, charismatic transformation of everyday life: in personal behaviour, interpersonal relationships, organizational processes, sociopolitical and ecological initiatives.

---

Perspective 17 is adapted from 'Spiritual inquiry as divine becoming' in *ReVision* (Heron 2001c).

# 18 On the way: a personal journal

From time to time I keep an occasional spiritual diary, as a way of clarifying, affirming and celebrating certain spiritual practices. Here is an unedited transcript of the original text, as written on the date of each entry, for one extended period of diary writing from 22 October 2001 to 18 April 04.

*A note on the chiaroscuro of the inner journal:* On the shadow side lurk the seductive anomalies of narcissism and inflated delusion. On the bright side there are the benefits of personal clarification, focused illumination and an affirmation of the inner life. More widely, there is a tacit invitation to dialogue and exchange perspectives with other inquirers on their own idiosyncratic paths. This silent dialogue of souls, to be fruitful, calls for the risks of intimate disclosure.

For two key overview entries see **14 May 2002** and **8 October 2002.**

## 22 Oct 2001

I stood on top of the pyramid this morning and talked up spiritual fire. I guess it's around all the time. When I speak out loud and open up to what there is in every respect without let or hindrance, the fire surges through and I become experiential flame. I stand and speak within physical space, embraced within subtle space, open to the origin of all this in what there is; and my-being-in-these-interpenetrating-spaces becomes an all-consuming, all-sustaining, all-creating everywhere active fire.

## 29 Oct 2001

Being in face-to-face relation to another person, with felt intimacy and mutual presence, opens up a field full of the potential for dynamic and world-transforming action - here in this place where we are.

## 30 Oct 2001

What's my basic world view, in a few short sentences? The divine is bipolar: spirit and manifestation. Spirit is bipolar: beyond the manifest and within the manifest, transcendent and immanent. The manifest is bipolar: the subtle and the phenomenal. Both the spirit and the manifest are one and many. Our intentionality in relationship in this situation here and now mediates and amalgamates this divine quaternary of polarities.

**3 Nov 2001**

The one taste, nondual state is a simple fusion of a developed state of witnessing, with the everyday state of feeling the presence of perceiving-a-world.

**10 Nov 2001**

I stand within our domestic pyramid, in its interior space, open my body-mind gesture to what there is in every respect without let or hindrance, and declare the word 'Fire'. Then I am aflame, a flame within the all flame, fiery all through.

**1 Feb 2002**

I made a mistake when sorting through my files, and lost a whole lot of journal entries between mid-November 2001 and the end of January 2002. What a pity, there were so many viable, illuminating entries. Such a shame! Oh well, I let them tumble away into nothingness, dissolve into the void. Frankly it was a bit of a struggle to let go of my attachment to journal-vanity and narcissism.

**2 Feb 2002**

Immanent spirituality manifests as the affective mode of the psyche, which involves a felt sense of fit in relation to the present situation, where this felt sense harbours a creative impulse to appropriate action, balancing the respective claims of the one and the many. See *Feeling and Personhood*, Figure 2.1, page 19, where affect is shown as embracing experiential and practical knowing.

**4 Feb 2002**

My current view is that the primary locus of human spirituality is situational, relational, co-created, dynamic and action-oriented. It is about the spiritual presence generated when humans interact with each other and their cultural and natural situation to transform their world - that is, to flourish in their world holistically. The dimensions of such interaction are communion, image-making, meaning-making, decision-making, and the varieties of conjoint transformative action.

This account of spirituality breaks down the distinction between spirituality, morality, psychology, politics, economics and ecology.

Co-creation involves a person in transformative transactions with elements of their own being relevant to the situation, with other persons involved, with other presences in the natural environment affected, with relevant norms, values and beliefs of their own culture, with human artefacts involved, with unseen presences and powers, with the divine as situational presence of this event.

The world peels off in layers from the exfoliating heart, of which You are the abundance and the fullness.

Action is an intrinsic ineffable knack of knowing how to co-enact, with the dynamic plethora of possibility, a new manifest determinate of the great indeterminacy of the divine.

### 7 Feb 2002

Parity is the primary value for humans. Parity between self-influence, peer-influence, up-hierarchy influence and down-hierarchy influence.

### 9 Feb 2002

More on parity. Parity meaning equal significance, giving equal weight to: not in any particular instance, but over time, in sequential balance. Today I may need to give greater attention to the value of up-hierarchy energies, tomorrow to down-hierarchy energies, on Monday to peer influence, and so on, but over time they all integrate into mutuality, harmony and balance – absolute parity.

Parity of ascent and descent, of vertical and horizontal, of the Many and the One.

I sat in my attunement chair for an hour and a half from 5.30 am this morning. A fairly regular practice at that time or earlier. It's a La-z-boy chair. You can raise up a support for the legs, and the back has about 18 different notches for reclining from the vertical to the near horizontal. Then seat and back recline together to maintain lumbar support. It's an excellent device for converting sleep into meditative attunement. This morning I attuned to the subtle worlds that are the ground and support, the very foundation, of the astral and physical cosmos. This supersubtle realm upholds our experiential world and its astral counterpart, and of course pervades them through and through. Physical existence gives a kind of privileged access to the everywhere intensive and extensive supersubtle. Just go down into your physicality and peer through it, look straight through what is in fact the rather slender veil of it, and there you are immersed in the all-pervasive supersubtle. Every good kitchen has a back door into an abundant garden whence it draws its nourishment. The body is the back door into the supersubtle, but it must be very relaxed and comfortable, and I alert and attentive, to pass through it. There is a certain notch on the chair which provides just the right angle of entry.

### 1 March 2002

The primary locus of human spirituality is situational - in this place with these people, in the collegiality, the diversity-in-unity, between the 'when' and the 'where' and the 'with whom'.

**28 April 2002**

We did a *Feeling and Personhood* exercise in the late afternoon. We took it in turns with the following. One of us read out sonorously a three sentence passage from the book about expansive feeling as the ground of the psyche, while Pachelbel's canon in D was playing in the background. The other relaxed deeply and openly, absorbing the sound of words and music, and letting the words echo for some more minutes until the music finished. Very nourishing. I indwelt an ocean of feeling out of which a pyramid arose, above whose apex a shimmering cloud of light extended.

**29 April 2002**

Sit in the La-z-boy chair from 5.50 am to 6.50 am. Then back to bed for some dreams. In the chair I dissociate into the uncreated, the unborn, the ultimate, the absolute, beyond all name and form, the simple, liberated space of awareness. This liberated space eventually always gently and warmly disavows the dissociation and settles down around the cosmic and psychological content which it both includes and transcends. To say it includes this content is not to say it is identical with it, it is just to say it includes it. Just like the ocean transcends and includes plankton, whales and such like.

**30 April 2002**

Sit in the chair from 3.50 am to 5.20 am. Open to the uncreate which settles in the heart, where layers of the create - the super-subtle, the subtle, the subtle-gross and the gross - peel off continuously in the ever-present, like contiguous petals emerging and unfurling. The subtle emerges from the super-subtle, the subtle-gross from the subtle, the gross from the subtle-gross, the gross disintegrates into the uncreate void, whence the super-subtle emerges, as the ever-present process continues. With these petals of the uncreate heart we feel our co-creative presence within our diverse realms of being.

Moving alone around the house during the day, I talk up experiential fire, the inextinguishable flame of being manifest. Interfused petals flaming round the uncreate.

In the evening about 7.15 pm, we do our cosmos ritual on the top of the pyramid, affirming our interconnection with the physical cosmos, the subtle cosmos and their spiritual ground. Then we take a candle each, one the light of Logos, the other the life of Shekinah, down staircases on opposite sides of the pyramid and process along a long passage from each end to meet in the middle of the pyramid. We place the candles on the low altar there and sit before it while a Tibetan bowl sounds its note. I open to the uncreate in the heart of each of us, and in the heart of every human on the planet. One race, one heart, one drama of multifarious unpeeling.

**10 May 2002**

I am in the chair for a couple of hours starting somewhere around 3 am, much earlier than usual. With my being I affirm emergently in many different ways the immediacy of You, Thisness, Thatness, What-there-isness. You as the Between, the I that integrates subject and object, my awareness and its immediate contents, in a seamless experiential whole of being. All sorts of stuff cascades within this seamlessness. Somewhere within this cascade a youth rushes eagerly toward me in some subtle realm.

In the early afternoon I stand in the middle of the pyramid and declaim aloud, "I open to what there is in every respect without let or hindrance". I make the declaration with the openness of my whole embodied being. This generates a blaze of experiential fire - a participation in the fiery breath of current creation. In terms of my model (Figure 6.1, page 95, *Sacred Science*) this experiential fire is an integration of my immediate present experience, its ground in its inner spatio-temporal matrix with its evoked constitutive fiery subtle energies, rooted in a deep impulse of immanent spiritual life, flaming in the air of sustaining universal mind, within the invoked creative outpouring of powers, presences and the transcendent Thou. So it is present experience integrated with immanent 1, 2 and 3, transcendent 1, 2 and 3.

**11 May 2002**

I go to the chair about 5.20 am for an hour or two. I simply attend to my attention, am aware of my awareness, although it's a bit more than that. I am aware of, and participate in, my living presence. Awareness of my awareness is nourished by my own living being. Divinity enjoys the feast it is serving up through my flesh.

**13 May 2002**

I sit in the chair from 5.30 am for an hour and a half. I spend some time opening to the ground, the foundation of my being, and of being - rootedness in the void. Then I open to the awareness, the free attention, that embraces our galaxy, the whole extended sphere of it, not just the central disc. The disc is some 10,000 light years thick, but the whole galactic sphere is 100,000 light years in diameter. Finally and for the greater part of the period in the chair, I settle into the following. I have in my being the silent speech "This is You" referring to my awareness with its immediate multi-layered experiential living content, and divinity. So this awareness of living content is You the divine. Awareness, life, multi-layering, content, You, me, there is no separation anywhere, no loss of distinctness nor of differential meaning anywhere.

Afterwards in bed I have a lucid dream. A shakti woman is driving the a small sedan car we are in backward, the wheels on our left graze the curb, then she pulls the car out into the road still going backwards. I am alarmed. I protest loudly, and fearfully, that we will crash. She does a U-turn careening round backwards down a road or lane that goes back to where we started. She manoeuvres the car round and parks it facing the same direction as before we started our backward trip. I notice a male passenger in the back; and also that there has been a miraculous transformation. I tell them that we are all in the same car, but that what for them it is still a closed sedan, is now for me an open sports car with no roof and windows and no windscreen - a vintage model called an Avis Minor (*avis*, Latin for bird). We are in the same car but from the vantage point of two different and interpenetrating realities, mine roofless, theirs roofed. When shakti finally parks the car, the front edge of the left front wing scrapes a little on a wall.

**14 May 2002**

I sit in the chair from 4.33 am to 6.33 am. The living thoughts - being thoughts – of silent speech, are windows, conduits to their referents. They are epiphanies: they commune with being. For a while I roam about divinity, exploring various thought-epiphanies, varied participatory approaches to, perspectives on, divine life-mind-manifestation. Then I settle on the thought-epiphany "This is You", referring, as before, to the divinity of Your-my awareness with its immediate multilayered experiential living content. I open to the spontaneous guidance of this epiphany. Today it takes me, over and over, in a series of cycles, into a third eye cone, a tunnel penetrating both upwardly and deeply into subtle space, which opens out at its end onto a world of spiritual intimates. Somewhere between these cycles, there is a phase where it is as if the top of my skull comes off, like a boiled egg with the top removed, and my brain is being flushed out with subtle energy.

Later in the day I reflect that this kind of spiritual and subtle experience, afforded within deep states of solitary meditation, especially in the pre-dawn hours, is secondary to what is afforded by relational forms of spiritual practice with other human beings. The solitary practice certainly deconstructs the contracted ego, opening it to the subtle and the spiritual. But this only deals with that part of the ego which is contracted against transpersonal realities. The sustained solitariness of such practice does nothing, per se, to deal with that part of the ego that is contracted against interpersonal collaboration. If anything, solitary meditation reinforces that sort of contraction by ballooning round it a subtle kind of inflation. Which is why traditional meditation gurus are notoriously unaware of the claims of ecumenical collaboration with each other, and are, in effect, in subtle competition for souls in the marketplace.

The interpersonal contraction of the ego needs dealing with at its own level, by acquiring competence in peer decision-making, followed by collaborative action, with regard to how we transform ourselves and our world. This kind of deconstruction of the ego is both fully interactive, incarnate, multi-level and holistic, engaging the subjective, the intersubjective, the social and the physical. Its rigours, including the rigours of chaos, burn up the privatized ego; its collegial creativity pours out rewards on all levels. And there are no traditions that teach it, because it necessarily transcends doctrinal transmission by authorized teachers. It's a new dispensation, only self-generated now by humans in this place.

Relational forms of spiritual practice, co-decided and co-exercised with other humans, seem to me to be primary, more fundamental than solitary forms. This is because they deal more radically and more comprehensively and more co-creatively with more of divine reality. Also interpersonal contraction is the toughest, thickest part of total ego contraction. If you deal with that really effectively, on all levels, you necessarily deal with the thinner transpersonal part. However, solitary forms of practice are a very important secondary back-up for dealing with this part.

**15 May 2002**

Instead of going by transcendence into the formless and then going on with it until it starts to subsume the phenomenal and turns into the so-called nondual (and leaves you devoid of all sorts of spiritual interactive skills), start with participatory perceiving grounded in the human capacity for feeling as I define it, practise this and expand this as a ground for developing emotional, interpersonal and psychosexual and other spiritual interactive skills, including above all peer decision-making and collaborative endeavour in world transformation.

**26 May 2002**

Consciousness is not experience. Experience is experience of being in a world; it's a composite of consciousness and life. Experience is sentience, feeling being in a world. It is developing, changing, becoming. Life is the motive power of this becoming. Consciousness as such is changeless, the great attractor.

Spirituality is not measured by high states, but by co-creative achievement. High states confuse the supersubtle with the spiritual.

You use revisionary concepts to release perceiving from the restrictive grip of traditional concepts.

Motion is the grounding form of life, animation.

## 18 Aug 2002

I've been away for five weeks to the USA and UK working and seeing family. Both activities have been rewarding, and yet what a pain to be away from my home here in NZ for so long.

How to live a life consciously, have a living consciousness, manifest a dipolar and tripartite theology. How to make relational forms of spiritual practice primary. What a joyful set of creative endeavours.

I've been vegetating for a week, spending every day getting my silent computer system up and running and tidying my desk. This has largely been done, so now the wider and deeper issues beckon: enlivenment, engagement, enlightenment.

*Enlivenment:* opening to present animation, the dynamics of eternal life, the everpresent fire of being.

*Engagement:* relational forms of spiritual practice – participative perceiving, mutual attunement with persons, participative decision-making, personal/social/planetary transformation.

*Enlightenment:* turning about in the everyday mind to universal mind.

## 17 Sept 2002

I'm wondering about the conceptual format of my experiential worldview. Divine animation on every level. Each body or sheath is alive in its own way. The physical body is alive in relation to its intake of air, food and water. The subtle body is alive in its relation to its engagement with the everywhere, everpresent subtle fire, the flame of subtle being, the eternal sheath of the divine. The supersubtle body is alive in relation to its taste of divine nectar.

## 18 Sept 2002

Theology and psychology again. Preconventional, conventional, postconventional and postpostconventional, these four as a model of personal development as we understand it today – this is OK.

## 19 Sept 2002

There's a flame in my heart. It's the flame of eternal life, divine animation. It lives forever and without end, within time and beyond time. It is the signature of immortality.

**6 Oct 2002**

I sat in the middle of the pyramid intoning aloud "YOU are the ground of my being" and opening the roots of my motivation to their divine ground, their spirit-animation. The result: a flow of fire upward from these roots.

One aspect of my personal path: to use the vibrational power of my voice to open my living being to the divine; and to use the metaphorical power of speech to open my awareness to the divine. Of course, spirit-animation is the vibrational power of my voice.

I am a living being and an aware being. My animation and my awareness are interdependent, co-relative. They are the dynamic poles of my entity. My animation is the sheath, vehicle, epiphany, manifest of my awareness. My awareness is the celebrant of my animation.

My primary sheath is immortal, that is, non-mortal. It combines transience and permanence. It is forever and it undergoes transfigurations and transformations. Transfigurations alter its frequency, transformations change its form.

My secondary sheath is mortal, my so-called physical body. I say 'so-called' because it is a temporary exudate of the primary sheath. It exists for purposes of training and learning, and for mastery of multi-domain living, that is for living awarely, creatively in several interrelated domains.

My primary sheath is a fire-body, a flame-body, a burning signature of entityhood. It is a glory of creation.

**7 Oct 2002**

Battling with fatigue, lack of sleep, overeating. I want to make some kind of statement about the sort of universe I live in and the range of practices I adopt.

**8 Oct 2002**

Nothing on the agenda for the day. Time to check in with the motivational ground of my being. I sit in the middle of the pyramid and say, with charismatic voice, "I open to the divine animation that is the root of my motivation".

Immediately there is an upward flow of fire from the root into the belly, the solar plexus and the heart; and a downward surge over each shoulder and down the back, like a descending cloak of flame. "O fire of agni, flame forever where I am."

Charismatic voice is the evocative power of human sound manifesting intent through transformative speaking. This mode of voice is like a wind that fans the flame of animate being.

For there is a kind of divine being that is animate, alive, moving, changing, doing things, constituting persons and worlds of all sorts and their transformations from and into each other.

Our inquiry group met last night. First off, a long discussion, with several rounds of voting, about an application from someone wanting to join the group. We decided to invite this person to attend for three meetings to test the waters, then to make a decision either to attend regularly as a committed member, or to leave; and group members would each make a response to whatever choice is made. Then we had a check-in round, each person reporting on whatever salient dynamic of their living they chose to share. After that, I brought in the basket of instruments and coloured cloths. For a long time there was vigorous rhythmic percussion – drums, rattles, cymbals, bells, wooden blocks, aboriginal pipe – with movement, gesture and posture, and no vocals. Then the sounding began, continuous and gentle until a pause. Next, with sacred dance and postures, a powerful multitone crescendo arose from group members. With devotional presence we sustained the fluctuating intensity of the interpenetrating sounds, with a series of crescendos and diminuendos. Other realities cascaded into the potentized prana of our physical and social space. Then at the final dying fall we sat in a silent circle hands linked, dwelling within the presence of Shekinah, feasting on the sweet nectar of the Divine Between: all in one, each in all, everywhere relationship, full of openness.

Now it is time to report on what Barbara and I have been doing since I got back here on 10 August from my five week trip to the USA and the UK. After two weeks of my taking it easy, we launched a three day review of our past and current process, and forward planning into the future. The review covered: (1) the many dimensions of our relationship; (2) our dyadic programme of shared practices; (3) prior lists of unfinished projects; (4) the purpose of the South Pacific Centre for Human Inquiry. The forward planning included: (1) personal, including holidays; (2) our dyadic programme of shared practices; (3) Centre activities and programme; (4) developing the grounds.

Under review (1), the many dimensions of our relationship, we reviewed all the following: our emotional dynamic; practical tasks; financial/legal/property; intimacy/nurturance/sex/togetherness; recreation; time together/time apart; decision-making; spirituality; families; TV; social life; age issues; food/exercise/sleep; intentional dying; careers/occupation; marriage; global viability. This review was very fruitful and rewarding as a living growth process: good strong, clear, open, rigorous and refreshing loving. It led over into a review of our past and current dyadic programme of shared practices. And this in turn developed into forward planning of the programme for the next three and a half months. We have at the time of writing been busy with the revised and extended version for five and a half weeks.

This dyadic programme is a programme of relational forms of spiritual practice. I think these really are primary in some fundamental way. The core practice is how we make decisions. On very many conjoint choices before us, however major or minor, we each first of all decide privately what our personal preference is, and only when both of us have got clear about this, do we disclose these preferences and in the light of these proceed to a negotiated shared decision. This has been a rigorous interpersonal discipline for many years, and may be exercised several times a day.

As well as being rigorous (we don't allow each other to avoid the first crucial step of determining personal preference), we keep it light, easy and playful. It is also intrinsically interesting and liberating. On matters large and small, we are continuously discovering who we are and where we stand. The process keeps the relationship sweet and clean, creative and respectful, and avoids collusion, control and muddling along. It ensures that co-operation is authentic and not cobbled together unawarely. It means that each person can check in with the deep inner ground of their motivation, to get a sense of where they truly stand as a basis for creative agreement. Thus immanent spirit is a spacious co-creative partner to the contract.

In our review of that process, we realized that there may have been a number of invisible decisions, not made in that way. 'Invisible' because they were made relatively unawarely in some other arbitrary manner. So we are intrigued to see if, in the future, we can spot these invisibles and identify how they are done and what it is about them that has made them invisible. I have to report that so far, five weeks on, either we haven't done any invisibles or we haven't spotted them. And to be honest, I'm not sure which of these is the case.

These are the names of all the other regular practices which we put into our forward plan for our dyadic programme, and which we have enjoyed over the past five weeks: mutual appreciation session, silent mutual gazing, the cosmos ritual in the house pyramid, the fire ritual in the glade, the ritual walk round the seats and sites, primary theatre, co-counselling, erotic energy declaration, identity check, *Feeling and Per-*

*sonhood* exercise, co-visualization. Interwoven with the plan are: grace at mealtimes, our conjoint decision-making process, and the sacred carnalities of erotic intimacy, and naked nurturance.

The mutual appreciation session is a joy: we take it in turns to celebrate a quality, a way of being or doing, that we appreciate about the other, up to a limit of three each – so we don't overdo it. What these six declarations and celebrations create is a very engaging and charming archetypal field, a spacious qualitative zone that opens up around us. We expand into the one mirror we each hold up for the other.

After the appreciations, we often do silent mutual gazing. As our souls settle into this enlivening process we become immersed in the dual-unity of Shekinah, the living open reality of the sacred Between. It's like being headless with two heads: only the Between savouring the unity of the duality. This mode of access to incarnate divinity really is so sweet, so rich in ambrosia. Why does not everyone use it? It is the true and universal form of *satsang:* peer to peer transmission of divine presence.

### 9 Oct 2002

I wander round the house, and I wonder round the house, saying "This is You", opening to what I see as what I AM, the unity of the whole subjective-objective process, all in one.

### 11 Oct 2002

Sludge, torpor, age, sloth, lack of sleep.

### 13 Oct 2002

Ditto.

### 14 Oct 2002

Last night we lay in bed in a naked embrace, close, flesh to flesh. In the shared silence, so pregnant with mutual regard, our souls spoke the unspoken words "We are You", our nurturance held in the spacious arms of divinity.

The performative, transformative use of language wells up out of the *hara,* the life centre in the belly. Co-creative, divine-human animation generates words, phrases and sentences that are transformative epiphanies: they manifest experientially their referents. They are Tantric doorways, windows, gateways, born of the marriage of life and mind, animation and awareness, shakti and shiva.

### 23 Oct 2002

We lie naked and close on the bed for an afternoon tropical siesta, the sweet passion of the Pacific ocean breaking gently on the shore a few metres away. As we merge into a luminous tactile highly alert swoon I feel our resonance with the archetypal ambrosia of a goddess and a god embraced within the unity of being. Shekinah of the South Pacific.

**28 Oct 2002**

We've been in a *fale* for nine days beside a long stretch of sandy beach at the north west end of Foa Island, Tonga, South Pacific. Every day we swim across a channel from the northern tip of Foa to a small uninhabited island immediately to the north. There's enough of a challenge for me to feel a tinge of the heroic: diverse reefs just below the surface, a westerly current whose strength varies with the cycle of the tides, and the distance across. The main business is snorkelling all the way over. I make my arm and leg strokes on the out breath, and breathe in the ocean prana through the hara as I glide through the tropical fish.

Sitting in a shaded grove on the edge of the beach after arrival, I feel the primordial unity of woman, man, earth, vegetation, sea and sky - a feast of orchestrated integration.

**9 Jan 2003**

I am all this here and now and the ground of it and the sky of it.

**10 Jan 2003**

All this behind the eyes where the inner and outer universes are one. Big one eye. Seeing in and out at the same time. Always big one eye.

**19 Jan 2003**

I sit in the chair for an hour and a half from about 3.45 am. I start opening to the divine creative word, the transcendent logos, then as the process of attunement and resonance continues, it slowly descends through my heart into the ground of all my primary energies, the divine ground of the life desires to circulate the blood, to breathe, stand, move, eat, drink, to be nurtured, be sexual, to hear, see, smell, taste and touch. I become infused with the deep indwelling godrich source of all human pleasure and excitement in being embodied.

**20 Jan 2003**

I go to the chair some time after 3 am for a while. I am taken with a threefold, tripartite attunement: of emergence, of presence and of emanation. I am open to the ground of my being, the rootedness of my embodied being and its desires and energies in the divine void, the womb of being; I am open to the everpresent jewel of OM in my heart; I am open to the emanation of my 'I' from the Logos, the divine creative word. Three in one, the realistic trinity: the ground, roots and stem of the lotus flower; the jewel within the lotus flower; the overshadowing effulgent light within which the lotus flower blooms.

Barbara returned yesterday evening from the Co-counselling International workshop. She had an envelope full of appreciations of her being, written on various sizes and shapes of special paper and card. What a feast for me to read. So many had realized who she is. I was lit up by the glow from these validations of her presence.

**24 Jan 2003**

I sit in the chair for 90 minutes from 3.30 am. I spend the whole time indwelling the life presence in the hara.

My teaching about spiritual practice is that there are three basic kinds of practice, and two modes of each kind. The three kinds are enlivenment, engagement and enlightenment; and the two modes are attuned reception and expressive action.

Enlivenment is about opening to and expressing the divine potential within the primary energies of our embodiment, that is, within the basic life impulses to breathe, stand, reach out, move, sleep, eat, drink, perceive, speak, relate, be sexual.

Engagement is about opening to and co-creatively expressing the divine presence that is the connectedness between us and other entities in this here and now situation.

Enlightenment is about opening to and expressing transcendent divine awareness and its refraction through powers and presences.

**28 Jan 2003**

I sit in the chair for about two hours from 3 am. I attend to the uncreate, the unborn, the spacious non-manifest, by penetrating the manifest veils of the physical, the subtle and the super-subtle. Of course they are veils when I seek to penetrate through them, or draw them open like curtains, to open to the uncreate. When I creatively and actively engage with them, then they are revelatory and dynamic epiphanies. The uncreate is a great openness in which all forms and processes reside, and which is unbound by any of them, and is the absolutely indeterminate correlate of their distinctiveness.

**30 Jan 2003**

I sit in the chair for 90 minutes in the early hours between midnight and pre-dawn. I enter the eternal vitality of the spiritual heart, dwelling in the ecstatic inner kindling of immortal flame. Everpresent life is fire.

**3 Feb 2003**

See *Sacred Science,* pages 249-250, for a full account of presence-as-such.

**5 Feb 2003**

Sit in the chair from 3.30 am for an hour or so. Simple tranquil intra-sensory awareness attunement. The physiological pleasure of total relaxation. Divinity of the tissues. Endorphin playground.

**10 Feb 2003**

Breathing in vital force from the archetypal body into the mediating body, breathing out vital force from the mediating body into the etheric envelope of the physical body.

**12 Feb 2003**

There is mortal vitality. And there is immortal, that is, nonmortal, vitality: vital force is the irreducible complement of awareness in the post death states. As an embodied being, I have access to physical vital force, to subtle vital force (of three different qualitative kinds), and to supersubtle vital force.

**13 Feb 2003**

Sit in the chair for an hour and a half pre-dawn, and lift off, subjectively, through the resurrections. Resurrection one: from the physical body to subtle body 1 within the individualistic postdeath realms. Thence to resurrection two: to subtle body 2 within the co-operative postdeath realms. Thence to resurrection three: to subtle body 3 within the transcendent postdeath realms. Thence to the great liberation of resurrection four: beyond the sublunary, bound realms of the postdeath journey, to the supersubtle body (subtle body 4) within the vast open empyrean spaces of the archetypal, supersubtle universe. Thence to resurrection five: to subtle body 5 within the embrace of the uncreate, the original one unborn being.

At the same time as going out from realm to realm, to the peripheral embrace of the uncreate, I am going in, peeling off corresponding petal sheaths around the heart, until the final fifth sheath opens inward to the infinitude of the uncreate within the heart.

**15 Feb 2003**

I sit in the chair for ninety minutes predawn, and attend fully, without respite, to the explosive divine potential of kundalini-shakti within the bodily fundament. It moves my bodily energies into a state of grace.

**18 Feb 2003**

I sit in the chair for ninety minutes or more predawn (ending at 5.24 am). After using several mantra doorways from the esoteric tradition of EBML – all of which open on potent avenues to the experiential divine

– I am consumed by the everpresent divine fire. I am a lambent flame within the here and now immortal fire of god.

**25 Feb 2003**

The spiritual potential within primary life energy: the inquiry approach through combined presentational and practical knowing, through creative artistic vital and imaginal action. Here are the steps I take:

The basic vital-imaginal action is to draw a highly animated line on the canvas (layer one in Adobe Photoshop). This is a line charged with *elan vital,* the 'rhythmic vitality' that is the classic aesthetic criterion of Chinese art. This is a line fraught with the Dionysian emergent presence in the creative act of drawing it. It is full of imaginal potential coded into the vital force of its emergence.

Integrate this line with its polar complement, an exact mirror image. I do this by making a copy of the line, pasting the copy into layer two, and flipping it horizontally, and positioning it as the symmetrical complement to the original line.

This integration of the original line and its polar complement may already reveal its imaginal, archetypal potential. A compelling image of life-forms and processes appears.

It may or may not be appropriate to enhance the resultant image by repeated the whole process on two more layers, layer three and layer four. These two bipolar forms are integrated together.

I merge all the layers into one composite image, and open my creative energies to the call of colour. The subjective-objective components parts of the image push their claims for their distinctive colouring.

I then apply one or more artistic effects to the whole image, to do with sources of illumination, brightness, contrast, colour control, gradients, texture, and so on. The purpose of these is to enhance its aesthetic impact and presence.

The basic evaluative criterion for the image is threefold: its rhythmic vitality, its presence, and its enhancement of awareness as a gateway, a Tantric opening, into the Shekinah between.

**1 March 2003**

I sat in the chair for 90 minutes before and including early dawn. Into the nirvana of the uncreate, whence outpours in sound and light the glory of the supersubtle, then the subtle, then the corporeal. This uncreate then traces its progeny in the very cells of the corporeal body. The uncreate is the ground of the cell, the heart of the cell and the open perimeter of the cell.

I can practice attunement to the divine in six ways, three in which the active will opens inwardly to the receptive, and three in which the receptive is ground to the active will opening outwardly to engage with the subtle, social and physical worlds.

The active will opening inwardly to the receptive:

- Especially predawn, opening to the transcendent uncreate and tracing its descending lineage as the ground of the manifest.
- During the day, opening to the divine presence that is the reality between all of us, the differentiated entities interacting and interconnected within this here and now situation where we are.
- During the day, opening to the impulses of divine animation that are the ground of our human motivation to act in this, that or the other way in our present situation.

The active will opening outwardly to engage with the subtle, social and physical worlds:

- Formulating and communicating visions of integral development for human beings.
- Engaging in a variety of co-operative practices with other persons and the biosphere.
- Manifesting idiosyncratic and authentic individual autonomous creativity.

**2 March 2003**

Time is the nature of becoming. It has three dimensions of simultaneity, duration and change, and the all-inclusive one of these is simultaneity. Becoming means being in a world of simultaneous events: events that occur at the same time. An event has duration, it lasts from before to after. And an event undergoes change: it is different after from what it was before. Simultaneity includes an explicit degree of duration and change, and an indeterminate tacit or subliminal degree of duration and change. To be aware of two events as simultaneous is to be aware of their concurrent duration and change manifest within a certain temporal limit.

**3 April 2003**

I live in the archnatural body through the immortality of the soul.

**15 April 2003**

Yesterday a full day of sluggish torpor.

**21 April 2003**

I open to what there is in the full incarnational praxis of entityhood.

**22 April 2003**

Incarnational praxis. The same as enlivenment. It means activating the incarnational being - through intentional upright and open posture, expansive gesture, charismatic power of voice and choice of words – to resonate with the totality of being, in every respect without let or hindrance. This activity converts the practitioner of it into participative experiential fire, the living flame of here and now divinity.

**9 May 2003**

Last night I slept for just over four hours, then did the following for just over three hours. I lay on my back in bed without moving, legs uncrossed, arms and hands out to the side. First I tuned in to, visualized and affirmed, all the body systems: bones, muscles, skin, cardiovascular, brain and nerves, alimentary canal and vital organs, endocrine. Second, I tuned in to, visualized and affirmed, the subtle matrix of the physical body, its energy centres, energy conduits. Third, I tuned in to, visualized and affirmed, the immortal flame sheath, the undying divine body. At the conclusion of all this, I rejoined the esoteric fellowship of mystic light. 'Esoteric' means 'intelligible only to those with special knowledge' and 'intended only for the initiated'. Any worthwhile science, of any kind, is esoteric in both these senses for serious practitioners of it. At the same time it entails an obligation among these practitioners to explain and apply its beneficial implications exoterically, and to make entry into its inner sanctum available for all who wish to acquire the appropriate skills.

**4 June 2003**

In the early morning, after a few hours sleep, I opened up to the fullness of the dark energy of my embodiment in the full process of divine becoming, the whole spatiotemporal matrix of our planet in its cosmic setting, especially the temporal form of our biosphere with its evolutionary diversity of its creatures and the unfolding coagulum of the human race and its multitudes of risen souls in the postdeath states. Mentally intoning 'divine' on the in breath, opening to the variety of beings within their extended temporal womb, and 'becoming' on the out breath affirming the developmental thrust of the whole.

**29 Oct 2003**

What are two basic shortcomings of the Wilber world view? (1) It is a category error to include the development of human souls within the concept of evolution. (2) Accounts of past human behaviour cannot properly be used to define what people ought to do in the future, nor to predict what they will do.

**12 Nov 2003**

Short on sleep last night.

**26 Jan 2004**

What guiding principles do I hold about human spirituality?

One principle is that of enlivenment (another two are those of engagement and enlightenment). It's to do with the development of immanent spirit, that is, spirit as indwelling spiritual life, spirit as the root motive force of all our living body-mind energies. This root motive force is bipolar: it is the will to live as a distinct individual, a unique idiosyncratic human entity; and it is the correlative will to live as a universal human participant in a multidimensional cosmopolis.

This evening eight members of our inquiry group met for the first time this year, after the summer break, although the others are still away on summer holidays.

**29 Feb 04**

**Arising**

This morning before the altar in our attunement room I open to my arising from the great space within the ground of what there is. Actually it is the great interconnected web of all of Us arising.

**2 March 04**

**Inquiry**

The path of inquiry calls attention to the divine as the wellspring of my will to live, as my present relation with whom and with what there is here and now in this situation, and as the transcendent source of my consciousness. In each of these three contexts, however, the 'my' becomes transformed into a translucent and participative distinctness within a wider unity.

**3 March 04**

**Divine root**

I sat in the chair later than usual - about 6.35 am - and opened downward to the divine root of my will to live, of the motive power in my bones and muscles, blood and guts, and brain - the three Bs.

**7 March 04**

**The Voice**

The divine speaks in the belly, in the hara. It is co-generated speech, the idiosyncratic language of mediated immediacy. I lay in bed in the early hours this morning giving linguistic shape in the belly to the Voice.

**Mortal gateway**

Divinity is the easiest of all things to know, and inescapably so. In the many-one universe with such a diversity of idiosyncratic entities, there are very many ways of diving knowing. The body is a great gateway: its stance, its movements and gestures - all they need is a little attitudinal tweak, a letting go of contraction and tension into all-around openness, to feel the living presence of the great space.

The mortal body is premised on the immortal body. To be in the mortal body in a certain kind of way - alert and relaxed, simultaneously present in all its parts, aligned and open in all directions in gesture and posture, free behind the eyes and spine - is to know its immortal premise, the fire body that is a universal participant in cosmopolis. Cosmopolis - the supersubtle first world of our indwelling.

**13 March 04**

**Dyadic review follow-up**

We got out all the detailed notes of the three-day review of our dyad which took place two and a half months ago at the end of December.

We transferred on to a wall chart all the individual and conjoint action-plans we had made at that time and pinned it on the outside of the bathroom door upstairs.

We then got fascinated by the uncompromising down-to-the bone devil's advocacy points, and by the greater or lesser rebuttals, which each of us had made to confront any degeneration and collusion in the quality of our relationship (of course there were also accessions). I wondered whether it would be fruitful to put all this into our *Cookbook of Dyadic Inquiry* as an addendum.

**14 March 04**

**Lambent flame**

I sat in our attunement room this morning and opened downward to the divine root of my motivation to live as a distinct entity and my motivation to live as a universal participant in cosmopolis. There's an upsurge of inner space and energy, a discreet fire, a flame. I look into the large mirror on the altar before me. First an aureole around the head and shoulders, then a lambent flame at the base of the spine, flickering upwards.

**Walk and glade**

We did our walk and glade ritual starting half past noon. Very leisurely: it took an hour and three quarters.

On the second seat, mutual gazing. On the fourth seat, mutual appreciations. In the glade, our fire and self-generating culture ritual. In the lower clearing in the bush, a smidgeon of co-counselling. In the dell, primary theatre. After the sixth and seventh seats on top of the hill, back to the altar in the centre of the house (also the centre of the pyramid) to close.

## 17 March 04

### Splendour

Walked round the house opening the fire-body, the immortal sheath, to its immersion in the interior universe, the first and most intimate body of the divine. What splendour shafts through these remarkable spaces.

## 28 March 04

Sat in the chair for an hour from 5.16 am, opening to Thou, the interior space, the pregnant void whence I emerge. The fullness, the nurturance of coming into being.

## 1-5 April 04

A five day co-operative inquiry with four colleagues from Oasis Centre in the UK and six of us from our Centre here. A remarkable breakthrough event, culminating in the morning of the final day in a transfiguring charismatic celebration of being. For a full ninety minutes we co-generate an extraordinary space, with diverse crescendos of tonal resonance, with varied patterns of percussive music, with a vast divine-human range of impromptu declarations and assertions, with exhilarating lightness and laughter, with many joyful verbal hallelujah-variations, with the participation of angel choirs, with our united archetypal roar of the divine wolf, and more and more, and forever and forever, the light-filled humour of an everlasting, ever open gracious space between.

## 18 April 04

Lying in bed pre-dawn I spent an hour or so mentally intoning 'we' on the in breath, while visualizing the whole interconnected web of life on the planet, human and non-human, incarnate and discarnate, in one great extended sphere merging into the super-subtle realms at the orbit of the moon; and intoning 'are' in the out breath, while visualizing a flame in an empty space at the centre of the sphere which was also in the centre of my being.

# 19 Coming into being

This Perspective tells the story of the start of the group which has continued its charismatic action inquiry, meeting every two or three weeks, for twelve years up to the time of my writing in 2006.

*Report status:* A story. *Place and year:* New Zealand, 1994-1997. *Spiritual focus:* Celebrating through improvised charismatic sound and movement our individual and interactive coming into being. *Subtle focus:* Exploring the range of subtle phenomena that support and enhance this celebration. *Social focus:* Affirming a group nucleus of holonomic spiritual activity and sustaining it within prevailing culture; injecting individual transpersonal activities into everyday culture; and creating a sub-culture of people intentionally inquiring into this kind of transpersonal social transformation.

## The evolution of the wavy group

In late 1993, some months after the Scott's Landing event described in Heron (1998: Chapter 13), I distributed a flyer among interested persons in New Zealand. It proposed, for February through April, 1994, a four day journey of opening, a co-operative inquiry into transpersonal activities in everyday life, a training for co-operative inquiry initiators, and the start of an ongoing seed group. It presented these events as aspects of a self-generating culture. No fees were to be charged.

The three workshops all took place, and the second of them, about transpersonal activity in everyday life, is described in detail in Heron (1998: Chapter 15). They proved to be links in a chain of events which started at Scott's Landing in March 1993.

Eight people who had been at Scott's Landing met each month thereafter to check in with each other and share significant life events. They joined the transpersonal activities in everyday life inquiry, February to April 1994, and, enlarged by new members from that, continued on as a self-directing peer group after it closed and I had returned to Italy. This was the ongoing seed group, anticipated in the flyer. It continued to meet regularly throughout the southern winter of 1994-5, sharing personal and transpersonal experiences in a spirit of inquiry.

When I returned to New Zealand in early November 1994 I joined this ongoing group and we elected, over the summer of 1994-5, to focus our inquiry on the process of coming into being now. Each person adopted an idiosyncratic approach to this, choosing some of form of mantra, meditation, affirmation, inner opening, centreing, postural alignment, continuous attunement, way of being present, ritual process, which attended to their continuous coming into being now.

> The theme adopted by the group was coming into being, affirming and celebrating this each day and observing the impact of this within our ordinary life. Over the years this has become a regular and powerful way of beginning my day and also a way of affirming myself within something new I am stepping into within ordinary life. So as a tool, a skill, I might say 'I affirm my coming into being in this world as a competent, skilful and balanced mediator and adjudicator', then tune in and evoke higher beings with these qualities and at the same time broaden my awareness with my eyes, to beyond this world, expand out the back and sides of my head, and feel into and breath in these qualities. (Barbara Langton)

We met every two weeks. The form of the meeting was variable, but usually contained these elements, including informal discussion of any of them:

- Settling in, and attuning to each other with hand contact, toning, mind-emptying and mutual resonance.

- This increasingly led over, after an early meeting in which we gave ourselves permission to become charismatically disinhibited, into an extended phase of improvised movement and toning. This was a slow, sacred, sinuous, interactive dance, with expressive gestures of the arms and hands, which established a potent field of subtle energy and spiritual presence. It was simultaneously empowered by co-coordinated harmonies of toning, with successive waves of crescendo and diminuendo. This combination seemed to well up out of our own coming to being now and to be both an expression and a celebration of it. It appeared to me to be marked by four phenomena:

  1. A sense of numinous presence in our midst, as if each was open to and expressive of immanent spiritual life within each and every other, and between all.
  2. A participative awareness of divine powers, archetypal energies of creation.
  3. A participative awareness of unseen presences, refracting these powers.
  4. Precision of beginning and ending: both the lift off and the closure of the process were exactly timed, the qualitative shift of subtle energy being noted by all. They were not ours to command, but a matter of our co-operative openness and at-

tunement to wider reaches of being and the movement of the spirit within.

- Each person shared their experience, over the previous three weeks, of using their way of attending to coming into being now, and the impact of this on their everyday life.

- Each person made a statement about how they intended to proceed for the next three weeks, whether using the same procedure, some modification of it, or some new procedure, or both.

- An act of closure, perhaps hand contact and silent attunement.

The experience of the coming into being inquiry that lead into the forma-tion of the wavy group was very strong for me. I remember at the time describing it as a spiritual awakening. The fortnightly participation in the group, linked by the daily practice of presencing, the experience of com-ing into being at every moment, at a daily morning meditation session, and throughout the day at random moments, seemed to open up a field that held me in a state of flow in relation to the world around me and the day to day work and relating I was engaged in. I had a strong sense of be-ing held by something greater than me, a sense of spiritual family, or a class of friends who were learning together, that was very often with me during the day and while asleep. It was a felt presence of the other people involved as a container, or field of activity.

The outcome in my life was a heightened sense of participating in an un-folding nature of being human in the world. The access into this aware-ness was assisted by the presence of, participation in, the field of inquiry held in place by myself and co-inquirers. (Rex McCann)

Because of its characteristic sinuous sacred dance, this group became known among its members as the wavy group. It met early one evening for the autumn equinox, in March 1995, at the bottom of the grass-covered crater within the summit of One Tree Hill in the centre of Auckland. As some fifteen of us gathered, we spread far apart over the grass, deep in the crater, and stood scattered and silent for a while. Then, as if suddenly called, we moved slowly into the centre and en-tranced ourselves with moving and toning, until the equinoctial hour had had its expressive say.

The more formal inquiry phase, of planning and reporting back on in-dividual practices used between group sessions, ended in April. The group continued to meet regularly throughout the southern winter and spring of 1995-6, to wave and weave together and otherwise interact.

A consistent core group continues to meet fortnightly for some personal sharing and then what for me is the rich, deep, sometimes mysterious emergence of a varying mixture of toning, waving, stomping, growling,

> sounding instruments, silent attunement, co-creating and speaking out of
> resonance with an archetypal form, subtle energies of a planet or a seem-
> ing felt sense of the divine. (Barbara Langton)

It continued on as a distinct strand, with some of the same members as,
and alongside, the empowerment in everyday life inquiry in the southern summer of 1996.

> I particularly enjoyed the sessions where we all allowed ourselves to play
> with energy in a light and joyful way trying out different movements and
> sounds. It was as if we were tapping into a very potent energy source.
> During 1994-6 the energy of the group seemed to imbue the rest of my
> life and when I think back to it I can contact the energy now. It is time-
> less. (Dale Hunter)

When that ended in April 1996, it continued to meet regularly throughout the southern winter and spring of 1996, with many variations of
format. For some weeks in the southern summer of 1996-7, it launched
a gender inquiry in which the women met each fortnight in their own
group, so too the men, and the combined groups met on the intervening
weeks. The ongoing group continues to meet as I write.

> This ongoing group has continued to provide a rhythm of a grounded
> spiritual attunement, a creative emergent unfolding from a shared felt
> sense of appropriate timing, and a natural elegance of form and pattern.
> Its Dionysian style creates an expansive space when we gather. And I feel
> that it works because of our shared experience with a more Apollonian
> formal co-operative inquiry, and because each individual is committed in
> their own life both to emotional and to transpersonal process. The space
> is such that we seem free to share our personal ups and downs and life
> process as well as transpersonal space. And we do review our process pe-
> riodically.

> Another aspect that has interested me is the ability and flexibility of the
> group to expand and reduce in numbers without losing these special
> qualities. Only one year I noticed some resistance of mine, to opening up
> to a larger group after the smaller core group had had a close intimate
> time through one winter. Although perhaps losing some of the familiar in-
> timacy, the richness of other people's energy and sharing easily balanced
> this for me. So it is as though a wider group who are part of it all for
> some months holds a container for the smaller group who meet more con-
> sistently throughout the year.

> For me its value and importance is in outwardly acknowledging and hav-
> ing spiritual space, sharing this with others in a way I find empowering
> and grounded, and maintaining a form that is open, varied, flexible,
> emergent from the people present, spontaneously creative, disinhibited
> charismatically to varying degrees, deeply nourishing, light, warm, sup-

portive and intimate. I find that it supports and enhances my own personal meditations and rituals. (Barbara Langton)

So four or six of us have been meeting, and its a new configuration so it's not clear yet what is emerging. We may need to redefine what we're doing. Roberta staunchly resists anything that sounds like stultified effort or intentionality. She complained that we have evolved a predictable format: a bit of greeting chatter, a check-in round, some toning and /or movement, leading to some silent attunement. That's true of course, but it doesn't bother me too much, the shape of the container the juice comes in. But I know I take this business of alignment seriously, so I'm prey to all the distortions that come from over-identifying with spiritual effort. Richard thinks we are simply arguing out the tension between Apollonian and Dionysian approaches. I think appropriate effort is the central issue in all spiritual endeavours, and I know there have been times in our groups when we were functioning with an openness in which there is no distinction between spontaneity and intentionality. Where I get caught is in thinking of these states as the real goods, and subtly resisting or manipulating what is, in order to achieve what is not. I suspect that's where Roberta smells a rat. I spent our last meeting letting go of all sense of responsibility for the experience of anyone else present, and letting go of any desire to be collectively generating any particular state of being. It's a liberating expansion into the present. (Glenn McNicoll)

## Evaluation

As I read it, the wavy group, in its several phases over the past four years, has been continuously inquiring, with highly flexible variations of format, into its own coming into being now. Its basic format is very Dionysian. It is more than adequate in terms of the broad sweep of its cyclic process, its total collaboration, its regular self-questioning (challenging uncritical subjectivity) and attention to emotional and interpersonal process. The inquiry is conducted in terms of a dynamic interplay between experiential knowing, presentational knowing, and practical knowing:

- The experiential knowing is of our coming into being now as persons in relation within the presence of Being and the surrounding field of interbeing.
- The presentational knowing is in symbolizing this radical knowing immediately in patterns of interactive sound and movement.
- The practical knowing, the knowing how, is twofold:
  1. The skill, in the expressive use of interactive sound and movement, to symbolize and participate in the process of divine creation.

2. The very subtle skill in managing congruence between the three forms of knowing, so that no one of them takes off on its own alienated from the other two.

The fundamental research cycling is the continuous interplay between the three kinds of knowing. This is religious action inquiry. Conventional action inquiry involves thinking (propositional knowing) in the midst of action (practical knowing). This more basic kind entails skilled action (practical knowing) that symbolizes (presentational knowing) opening to our coming into being (experiential knowing). In this sort, the element of celebration, of ecstatic abundance, evident in skilled presentational expression is prior to, is wider and deeper than, the element of inquiry its symbolism embraces.

The research cycling becomes more complete when it is extended to include phases of conceptual reflection. There is a great deal of virtue in delaying this phase for a long while. This is partly because in our culture it is very easy for such reflection to become rapidly dissociated from its relevant experiential base, and thus to disregard, denigrate or deny it. It is also because the interplay of the other three kinds of knowing in religious action inquiry needs a substantial period of ripening and maturity before it can provide a stable foundation for reflective inquiry.

---

Perspective 19 is the text of Chapter 20 in *Sacred Science* (Heron, 1998).

# 20 Into the future

## Just a start

The short-term co-operative inquiries of a few weeks or months represent a first bathe in the spiritual inquiry pool. Their outcomes in terms of transformations of being and transpersonal skills are a matter for each individual co-inquirer to declare. I have found them deeply transformative in opening to the immanent spiritual life within, and in adopting forms of charismatic, expressive and interactive spiritual practice that constitute authentic transfiguration.

In these early days the overall impact of the method is for many people an important transformational outcome, as much as any particular outcome to do with the focus of a given inquiry. This impact is about spiritual self-discovery, about the affirmation of internal spiritual authority, of autonomous creativity in choosing and following a spiritual path. It is about the intimate connection between indwelling spirit and open inquiry, between inner liberation and mutually respectful, co-operative, spiritual exploration with other persons.

For me the impact of the method is an affirmation that spiritual authority is within, contextually located, maculate and self-revising, that it guides our spiritual path in liberal association with others, that it is inalienably central to human spirituality, and that it is indeed in its very nature a form of divine becoming. Spiritual transformation, as I now see it, is about creative spiritualization of the person and personalization of the spirit, in the context of collaboratively taking charge of our planetary estate within the cosmic whole.

## Theological stripping

I think the method, applied to the spiritual field, presupposes and gives expression to a radical theology of the sort I have alluded to throughout this book. Others, however, may disagree with this theology, while wanting to use and apply the method within their own framework of religious belief. By this kind of theological stripping and reclothing, the method can be taken into any spiritual school for long-term inquiry into its fundamental beliefs and practices.

What this process will challenge, of course, is any controlling, hierarchical authoritarianism within the school. Such authoritarianism, in my view, rests on an unacknowledged insecurity within the teacher about the validity of the beliefs and practices he teaches to others; or, to put it another way, on the projected denial of his own internal spiritual authority. Where such authoritarianism is intransigent, accomplished practitioners within the school can set up their own autonomous peer inquiry group.

Religious traditions do in fact have a slow, grinding, cautious, unacknowledged kind of inquiry going on, a 'living hermeneutic process' (Vroom, 1989), sometimes schismatic, in which new experiences and insights lead to revisions of doctrine and practice. My proposal is simply that this living hermeneutic process is made more explicit, intentional, focused, and liberated from the arbitrary constraints of reactionary conservatism.

## Advantages and disadvantages

The methodological advantages of co-operative inquiry into the spiritual and the subtle are that the co-inquirers are able to:

- Devise practices consonant with their inner light and life, and give form to their own original relation to creation.

- Elicit categories of understanding appropriate to their experience, without relapsing unawarely into traditional doctrines, new age euphoria, or culturally prevalent beliefs and values.

- Sustain critical subjectivity by the use of inquiry cycles and validity procedures.

- Clarify practical issues about entering and exiting from the experience.

- Winnow out criteria for distinguishing spiritual experience from purely psychological or subtle states.

- Manifest, as central to the inquiry process, charismatic transformation of everyday life: in personal behaviour, interpersonal relationships, organizational processes, and sociopolitical initiatives.

The primary disadvantage, as with co-operative inquiry in any field, is consensus collusion, that is, uncritical intersubjectivity: people unawarely conspiring together to sustain gratifying illusion, false premises, spurious method. This can be interwoven with research countertransference: fear, triggered by the inquiry topic or process or both, is neither owned nor dispersed, and thus distorts what goes on in both the reflection and action phases.

Consensus collusion needs to be confronted and interrupted by the sensitive and searching use of a devil's advocacy procedure at appropriate times. While research counter-transference calls for time out to deal intentionally, by agreed methods, with the emotional distress stirred up.

A particular disadvantage in the spiritual and subtle field is that short inquiries of a few days or a few weeks or a few months do not constitute any kind of sustained practice. Nor do they provide the ongoing support, fellowship and collegial spiritual power of an established school. One solution to this already exists for those who follow their own self-directed path of lived inquiry, where this includes selective, discriminating affiliation with one or more schools of practice. Another solution lies in establishing autonomous peer groups for long-term spiritual practice within the self-generating spiritual culture from which co-operative inquiry itself has emerged, as described in this Perspective. Such groups are likely to have the following features:

- They are self-directed peer groups: there is no leader or long-term facilitator.

- They are clear and intentional about how they make decisions.

- They are founded on the practice of open inquiry: they work in the spirit of inquiry, without following formalized inquiry procedures.

- They attend to emotional and interpersonal processes as and when needed.

- They are vigilant about uncritical subjectivity: they periodically review their assumptions and procedures.

- They are innovative, risk-taking and disinhibited within the group: they are open to present impulses of immanent spiritual life, and present illuminations of transcendent spiritual consciousness.

- They are committed to transformative activities in everyday life outside the group.

- They engage once or twice a year in short-term formal and focused co-operative inquiries as a complement to their long-term practice.

This proposal for establishing such groups for long-term spiritual practice is not a lurch back into the old business of founding another authoritarian tradition. Neither I nor anyone else can set themselves up as an external authority who defines the nature of internal authority for other people. It is logically impossible to be authoritarian about the nature or the practice of internal authority, for by definition internal authority cannot be internal if it is commanded by someone else.

No-one can practise internal authority, exclusively by following an external authority who prescribes what it is: self-direction cannot be other-directed. Autonomous people cannot dictate the nature of autonomy for others; they can only dialogue and co-operatively inquire with each about the nature of self-direction.

Any self-directed peer group, whose early destiny was grounded in the internal authority of its members, and whose future members start to ground it on appeals to the authoritative statements of the founding members, as disclosed in old records, has lost its way and stumbled into *mauvais foi.*

The great political advantage of religious co-operative inquiries is the democratization of human spirituality, which has since recorded time been defined and controlled by imposed authority. Ordained authority figures have, in the name of god or the gods or spirits or ancestors or the tribe or the church or the lineage or the tradition or the scriptures or the living perfected master, told the rest of humanity what their spirituality is and how to express and develop it in practice. This is still the case today across the whole range of spiritual teachings from traditional religions, East and West, to channelled entities and new age gurus. As new cults, creeds and types of practice spring up today in great abundance, the founder of each immediately claims some form of authority to legitimate its teaching and win adherents.

Any spiritual school or tradition that claims any kind of external authority for its spiritual teachings and practices will seduce, disregard or downgrade human autonomy and its internal authority expressed as critical subjectivity, independent judgement, individual discriminating practice, inner-directed unfoldment, personal freedom of spirit in defining spiritual reality and in choosing and shaping the spiritual path.

When human beings join together to support each other, and find collective power, in fully respecting each other's internal authority, then, I surmise, a radically new theology may well emerge. It may perhaps affirm, not the primacy of redemption or salvation or enlightenment or release or emptiness or god-realization, for all these things appear to have been promoted to maintain the mediating role of authority figures. It may celebrate, by contrast, the primacy of charismatic practice, of co-creative engagement with divine doing and becoming, found where autonomous humans co-operatively inquire into world-transforming skills within their universal estate. It may not be meditation and prayer that stand at the forefront of spiritual practice. The paramount path may be the creative work of the collaborative cosmic citizen, for which interior transfiguration hones the assiduous blade.

---

Perspective 20 is adapted from the epilogue to part 2 in *Sacred Science* (Heron, 1998).

# References

Abram, D. (1996) *The Spell of the Sensuous.* New York: Vintage Books.

Alexander, C. (1979) *The Timeless Way of Building.* New York: Oxford University Press.

Alli, A. (2003) *Towards an Archeology of the Soul,* Berkeley, CA: Vertical Pool.

Baldwin, C. and Linnea, A. (2000) *A Guide to PeerSpirit Circling,* Langley, WA: PeerSpirit Inc.

Bateson, G. (1979) *Mind and Nature: A Necessary Unity.* New York: Dutton.

Battista, J.R. (1996) 'Offensive spirituality and spiritual defenses', in B.W. Sutton, A.B. Chinen and J.R. Battista (eds) *Textbook of Transpersonal Psychiatry and Psychology.* New York: Basic Books.

Baum, A. J. (1953) *Philosophy: An Introduction,* Chapter 20.

Bauwens, M. (2006) 'Peer to Peer and Human Evolution'. http://integralvisioning.org/article.php?story=p2ptheory1.

Berdyaev, N. (1937) *The Destiny of Man.* London: Ayer.

Berman, M. (1981) *The Reenchantment of the World.* Ithaca, NY: Cornell University Press,

Bernasconi, R. (1995) 'Maurice Merleau-Ponty', in T. Honderich (ed) *Oxford Companion to Philosophy.* Oxford: Oxford University Pres. pp. 554-555.

Bruteau, B. (1997) *God's Ecstasy: The Creation of a Self-Creating World,* New York: The Crossroad Publishing Company.

Buber, M. (1937) *I and Thou,* Edinburgh: Clark.

Burtt, E.A (1927) *The Metaphysical Foundations of Modern Science.*

Campbell, J. (1996) *Traveler in Space: In Search of Female Identity in Tibetan Buddhism.* New York: George Braziller.

Crook, J. (1996) 'Authenticity and the practice of Zen', *New Ch'an Forum,* 13: 15-30.

Durckheim, K. Graf Von (1962) *Hara: The Vital Centre of Man,* London: George Allen and Unwin.

Ferrer, J. (1998) 'Conocimiento transpersonal: una aproximacion epistemica a la transpersonalidad', in F. Rodriguez (ed) *Psicologia y Psicoterapia Transpersonales.* Barcelona: La Liebre de Marzo. English version in *Transpersonal Knowledge.*

## 158  Participatory spirituality

Ferrer, J. (2002) *Revisioning Transpersonal Theory: A Participatory Vision of Human Spirituality.* Albany, NY: SUNY Press.

Ferrer, J. N. (2003) 'Integral Transformative Practices: A Participatory Perspective', *The Journal of Transpersonal Psychology*, 35(1), 21-42.

Ferrer, J. N. (2006) 'Embodied Spirituality: Now and Then', *Tikkun: A Critique of Politics, Culture & Society.*

Gangaji (1995) *You Are That.* Novato, CA: Gangaji Foundation.

Gendlin, E. (1981) *Focusing,* London: Bantam Press.

Govinda, L.A. (1960) *The Foundations of Tibetan Mysticism.* London: Rider.

Green Party of Utah (2002) 'A happy 'how to' of formal consensus decision-making' at http://www.greenpartyofutah.org/

Grof, S. (1988) *The Adventure of Self-Discovery,* Albany, NY: SUNY Press.

Hanh, T. N. (1995) The Heart of Understanding. Berkeley, CA: Parallax Press.

Hartshorne, C. and Reese, W. (1953) *Philosophers Speak of God.* Chicago: University of Chicago Press.

Heron, J. (1971) *Experience and Method.* Guildford: University of Surrey.

Heron, J. (1981a) *Paradigm Papers.* London: British Postgraduate Medical Federation.

Heron, J. (1981b) 'Experiential research methodology', in P. Reason and J. Rowan (eds) *Human Inquiry: A Sourcebook of New Paradigm Research.* Chichester: Wiley.

Heron, J. (1984) 'Holistic endeavour in postgraduate medical education' in *The British Journal of Holistic Medicine,* 1:1, 80-91.

Heron, J. (1988) 'Assessment revisited' in Boud, D. (ed) *Developing Student Autonomy in Learning.* London: Kogan Page.

Heron, J. (1992) *Feeling and Personhood: Psychology in Another Key,* London: Sage.

Heron, J. (1996a) *Co-operative Inquiry: Research into the Human Condition.* London: Sage.

Heron, J. (1996b) 'Helping Whole People Learn' in Boud D. and Miller N. (eds), *Working with Experience: Promoting Learning.* London: Routledge, 1996.

Heron, J. (1997) 'A Self-generating Practitioner Community' in R. House and N. Totton (Eds), *Implausible Professions: Arguments for Pluralism and Autonomy in Psychotherapy and Counselling,* Ross-on-Wye: PCCS Books.

Heron, J. (1998) *Sacred Science: Person-centred Inquiry into the Spiritual and the Subtle,* Ross-on-Wye: PCCS Books.

Heron, J. (1999) *The Complete Facilitator's Handbook,* London: Kogan Page.

Heron, J. (2001a) 'Transpersonal co-operative inquiry', in H. Bradbury and P. Reason (eds), *Handbook of Action Research,* London: Sage. pp. 333-339.

Heron, J. (2001b) *Helping the Client: A Creative, Practical Guide*, London: Sage.

Heron, J. (2001c) 'Spiritual Inquiry as Divine Becoming', *ReVision*, 24:2. 32-41.

Heron, J. (2006) *Living in Two Worlds.* Auckland: Endymion Press.

Heron, J. and Lahood, G. (2008) 'Action research in the realm of the between' in H. Bradbury and P. Reason (eds), *Handbook of Action Research*, second edition, London: Sage Publications. Forthcoming.

Heron, J. and Reason, P. (1985) *Whole Person Medicine: A Co-operative Inquiry.* London: British Postgraduate Medical Federation.

Heron, J. and Reason, P. (1997) 'A participatory inquiry paradigm', *Qualitative Inquiry*, 3(3): 274-294.

Heron, J. and Reason, P. (2001) 'The practice of co-operative inquiry', in H. Bradbury and P. Reason (eds), *Handbook of Action Research*, London: Sage. pp. 179-188.

Houston, J. (1987) *The Search for the Beloved.* Los Angeles: Tarcher.

Hubbard, B. M. (1998) *Conscious Evolution: Awakening the Power of our Social Potential*, Novato, CA: New World Library.

Hyde, L. (1949) *The Nameless Faith.* London: Rider.

Katz, S.T. (1978) 'Language, epistemology, and mysticism', in S. Katz (ed) *Mysticism and Philosophical Analysis.* New York: Oxford University Press.

Kelly, G.B. (1993) *Karl Rahner: Theologian of the Graced Search for Meaning.* Edinburgh: Clark.

Kitselman, A.L. (1953) *E-Therapy.* New York: Institute of Integration.

Kramer, J. and Alstad, D. (1993) *The Guru Papers: Masks of Authoritarian Power*, Berkeley: Frog Ltd.

Lachs, S. (1994) 'A slice of Zen in America', *New Ch'an Forum*, 10.

Langton, B. and Heron, J. (2003) *Cookbook of Dyadic Inquiry*, www.human-inquiry.com/cookbook.htm.

Leonard, G. and Murphy, M. (1995) *The Life We Are Given: A Long-term Program for Realizing the Potential of our Body, Mind, Heart and Soul*, New York: Tarcher.

Maslow, A. (1970) *Motivation and Personality.* New York: Harper & Row.

McMahon, E. and Campbell, P. (1991) *The Focusing Steps.* Kansas City, MO: Sheed and Ward.

Merleau-Ponty, M. (1962) *Phenomenology of Perception.* London: Routledge and Kegan Paul.

Monroe, R.A. (1972) *Journeys Out of the Body.* London: Souvenir Press.

Panikkar, R. (1996) 'A self-critical dialogue', in J. Prabhu (ed), *The Intercultural Challenge of Raimon Panikkar.* Maryknoll, NY: Orbis Books. pp 227-291.

Peat, F.D. (1996) *Blackfoot Physics.* London: Fourth Estate.

Peat, F.D. (1997) *Infinite Potential: The Life and Times of David Bohm.* New York: Addison Wesley.

Raphael, M. (1994) 'Feminism, constructivism and numinous experience', *Religious Studies,* 30: 511-526.

Reason, P. (1988) (ed) *Human Inquiry in Action.* London: Sage.

Reason, P. (1994) (ed) *Participation in Human Inquiry.* London: Sage.

Reason, P. (ed) (2002) Special issue, 'The Practice of Co-operative Inquiry', *Systemic Practice and Action Research, 14*(6).

Reason, P. and Bradbury, H. (eds) (2001) *Handbook of Action Research.* London: Sage.

Reason, P. and Rowan, J. (eds) (1981) *Human Inquiry: A Sourcebook of New Paradigm Research.* Chichester: Wiley.

Rogers, C. (1959) 'A theory of therapy, personality, and interpersonal relationships, as developed in the client-centred framework', in S. Koch (ed) *Psychology: A Study of a Science,* Vol 3. New York: Penguin.

Rogers, C. (1980) *A Way of Being.* Boston: Houghton Mifflin.

Romero, M. T. and Albareda, R. V. (2001) 'Born on earth: sexuality, spirituality and human evolution', ReVision, 24: 2, 5-14.

Rothberg, D. (1986) 'Philosophical foundations of transpersonal psychology: an introduction to some basic issues', *Journal of Transpersonal Psychology,* 18(1): 1-34.

Skolimowski, H. (1994) *The Participatory Mind.* London: Arkana.

Spretnak, C. (1991) *States of Grace: The Recovery of Meaning in the Postmodern Age.* San Francisco: Harper-Collins.

Spretnak, C. (1995) 'Embodied, embedded philosophy', *Open Eye,* California Institute for Integral Studies, 12(1): 4-5.

Tarnas, R. (1991) *The Passion of the Western Mind: Understanding the Ideas That Have Shaped our World View.* New York: Ballantine Books.

Trimondi, V. and Trimondi, V. (2003) *The Shadow of the Dalai Lama,* www.trimondi.de

Varela, F. J., Thompson, E. and Rosch, E. (1991) *The Embodied Mind: Cognitive Science and Human Experience.* Cambridge, MA: MIT Press.

Vroom, H.M. *Religions and the Truth: philosophical Reflections and Perspectives.* Grand Rapids, MI: William B. Eerdmans.

Washburn, M. (1995) *The Ego and the Dynamic Ground: A Transpersonal Theory of Human Development,* Albany, NY: SUNY Press.

Washburn, M. (2003) *Embodied Spirituality in a Sacred World.* Albany, N.Y.: SUNY Press.

Whitehead, A.N. (1926) Science and the Modern World. Cambridge: Cambridge University Press.

Wilber, K. (1990) *Eye to Eye: The Quest of the New Paradigm.* Boston: Shambhala.

Wilber, K. (1995) *Sex, Ecology, Spirituality: The Spirit of Evolution,* Boston: Shambhala.

Wilber, K. (1997) *The Eye of the Spirit.* Boston: Shambhala.

Wilber, K. (2000a) *Integral Psychology.* Boston: Shambhala.

Wilber, K. (2000b) *One Taste: Daily Reflections on Integral Spirituality.* Boston: Shambhala.

Yorks, L. and Kasl, E. (eds) (2002) *Collaborative Inquiry as a Learning Strategy.* San Francisco: Jossey-Bass.